Falling in Love with Yourself. The Key to Ending Anxiety and Depression.

BEATRIZ E. MUSICK

Copyright © 2019 Beatriz E. Trevino

All rights reserved.

ISBN: 978-0-9982520-2-5

DEDICATION

"Being me, the most scary but amazing adventure that set me free".

This book is dedicated to every human in the entire planet struggling with low self-esteem, therefore, depression and anxiety.

Disney and Religion lied to us all. There is no prince charming coming to save you, save yourself.

CONTENTS

- **1** Getting to know your inner child.
- **2** Becoming one with your inner child.
- **3** It's the parent who needs to change.
- **4** The backward roles.
- **5** The fear of being selfish.
- **6** Who said you were naked?
- **7** Manifesting Heaven on earth.
- **8** What is perfectionism?
- **9** Our life mirrors our own belief system.
- **10** Fully acceptance of our bodies.
- **11** Childhood -elementary years –.
- **12** Utopia meditation, ages 0-7 years.
- **13** Our relationships mirror our self-esteem.
- **14** Getting our passion back.
- **15** Accepting our sexuality.
- **16** Utopia meditation, age 8-14 years.
- **17** Letting go of unhealthy relationships and old belief systems.
- **18** Making our dreams come true.
- **19** What about anger?
- **20** Utopia meditation, ages 14-21.
- **21** Do we really, really love ourselves?
- **22** Forgiving, letting go of all resentment.
- **23** Dealing with shame.
- **24** Vulnerability
- **25** Focusing on the positive.
- **26** Irrational fears.
- **27** Do we ever fully recover or do we just manage it?
- **28** Utopia meditation, ages 22-33.
- **29** Can you say "no" and not feel guilty?
- **30** Healthy communications.
- **31** Utopia meditation, Throat chakra balanced.

- **32** Intuition
- **33** Opening the mind.
- **34** Become the observer.
- **35** Living in the now.
- **36** Are we all psychic?
- **37** What is a higher dimension?
- **38** Learning to work with energy
- **39** Third Eye Chakra – Balanced – Utopia meditation
- **40** The Crown Chakra
- **41** One Life, not two; one body not two
- **42** Utopia Meditation
- **43** The end of the journey
- A note from the editor.

FALLING IN LOVE WITH YOURSELF

INTRODUCTION

This is my story. This is how I saved myself from my mind, how I went from misery to effortless love, joy and peace. It is meant to be used as a guide/workbook; you can skip chapters or go in any order. However, I suggest you follow the first few chapters in order to get you on the right track.

This process is going to be more helpful if you do it with others or as a group study book. I am sure that the support from others will definitely help. If you do not feel that the chapter is done, stay with it. Share amongst each other what you are learning and what is keeping you from moving forward. If you have no one to do it with, it is perfectly ok to do it alone. Do not forget I am here to help. You may want to contact me online: www.facebook.com/beatriz.musick

Each chapter contains an exercise/meditation. If you have never meditated, do not be afraid. Meditation is nothing more than quieting our mind so we can listen to our heart/spirit that knows it all and will eventually set us free. The truth always sets us free.

For those of you who do not know how to meditate. Here is a simple guide that might help you.

- Sit down, close your eyes and deep breathe three or more times. Until you feel the extra oxygen in your body and a sense of being relaxed. Begin to relax your body with every breath. Start by focusing and consciously relaxing your forehead,

your face, jaw, followed by the neck. Then focus on relaxing your shoulders. Continue consciously relaxing your entire body, from top to bottom. My suggestion is to always do it in a sitting position with your back straight. This will help to not fall asleep.
- Using your imagination, create/visualize a place/location of your own. No limitations. See yourself in that place, then visualize a door and wait for someone "that knows all your answers to your struggles" to show up. Many people envision Jesus, again no limitations here. Whatever works for you is fine.
- This is a very loving person that is all Wisdom. He or she is the representation of your own spirit. He knows all truth that will set you free. Allow this person to show love. No limitations – imagine/visualize whatever feels good to you.
- Ask him or her anything you want to know and then listen. Most likely a message will come to you as thoughts or ideas; it could also come to you in words. During meditation there is no right or wrong ever. That is your spirit/heart talking.
- You can see this person healing your soul, or/and your body. Let his/her light heal you. Stay here as long as you desire. Again, no right or wrong. The purpose is to enjoy yourself and be in touch with your own spirit/heart.
- If his/her message gave you an overwhelming sense of peace, that's it. You just became an expert at meditation.
- There is no right or wrong way of meditation. Many use focusing on their breathing to achieve the altered state of the mind. I mostly use my imagination. Repeating mantras, prayers, praying in tongues or even driving a vehicle are also ways

of keeping the left hemisphere of our brain busy, so we can listen within using our right hemisphere. There are plenty ways to learn. Do not be hard on yourself and enjoy.

When I refer to our parents, it does not necessarily mean your mom and dad. It could be any adult that parented you during your childhood.

Who is the inner child? It is not your thinking and it is not your body. Maybe we shouldn't even call it an "it". Your inner child is your higher or truer self. The one we really are, before all mind programming by caregivers and/or society. Now let us have fun healing ourselves.

These exercises were not meant to do one a day. Each step can take a week or even a few weeks. I suggest not moving on to the next chapter/exercise until you feel total peace and can effortlessly visualize what you are asked to see. Do not be discouraged, it is small baby steps in the right direction what we are looking for.

Know that most of us trained ourselves to block our feelings in order to survive or not feel overwhelming pain at some point in our lives. So once again, do not be so hard on yourself. Setting our feelings free is beyond scary and overwhelming for most. Be patient and know it will be a process.

1 GETTING TO KNOW YOUR INNER CHILD

What is LOVE anyway? Love is the decision to unconditionally respect and appreciate ourselves and therefore others. Unconditional love is nothing more than lack of judgment. Sounds hard? It is. Our brain has been trained to judge right or wrong (good and evil) at all times.

How many of us can freely say that we love ourselves without judgment? It was not until my late forties that I began to radically love myself. I believe that the main reason I had such a hard time loving myself is because of what was recorded in my subconscious mind early in life. I deeply believed that only perfection could be loved and I definitely did not consider myself anything close to perfection.

What is perfection anyway? I dedicated my entire youth trying to be perfect. Or better said, what I **thought** perfection meant. Later in life I learned that every single human has a different perception of what perfection is. But either way, I spent decades and all my energy trying to be whoever I **thought** perfection was. This created the most horrible dissonance or separation with my one true self or inner child. I stopped allowing the inner child to be who she was and began trying to change her into whomever I **thought** she needed to be. This is where the nightmare and low self-esteem began.

This dissonance effortlessly began to create fear, anxiety, depression and all sorts of low vibe feelings creating an endless cycle. The more I tried to be perfect, the less I could. Little did I know that I was born perfect and all I had to do was to be me.

As a result of this dis-attachment with my heart and my inner child, I developed an anxiety disorder including panic attacks, low energy and a cruel eating disorder.

To make matters worse, I was taught that god was a perfect god, therefore I concluded that he could only love perfection. So how was he going to love me, a wretched sinner? That is what religion told me over and over again. In my opinion, religion played a huge part in my low self-esteem and taught me to not listen or follow my own heart and feelings. We heard over and over to ignore our feelings and to live by what the mind said and never to be led by our feelings, since we were such sinners who desired only to sin.

The process we are about to begin today, is a process of getting ourselves connected back with our hearts and feelings and allowing our spirit/heart to lead us. This is a process of ending the deadly path, the mind led life that continued to produce hell on earth or self-destruction.

Many of us chose to avoid feeling in order to survive at some point in our lives and in order to continue to numb ourselves and not feel we might have ended with an addiction. However: it is never too late to go back and connect with our heart, even if it is a few decades later. So hang on and enjoy your ride to your heart.

ACTIVITY 1

For the next couple of days, you would close your eyes, twice a day and get in touch with your abandoned inner child. Why are we going to do this? Chances are that whoever parented you, abandoned you as a child. It doesn't necessarily mean that you were physically abandoned, maybe simply tried to change you into what they **thought** you needed to be and oppressed or emotionally abandoned the real you. I happen to believe that every child came into this life with a perfect blueprint of who we are and meant to do, but well intentioned parents or caregivers (guided by their minds) began trying to change us into what they **thought** we needed to be and do in this life time, for our own good, they **thought**.

We cannot go back to the past and change our parents. Hey, we can't even change them now. The fact is that it is us as adults abandoning ourselves now. We learned from our own parents how to parent our inner child and we learned well and continue to repeat the same story in our minds. We somehow ended up being our own worst enemies. We are so hard to ourselves and we continue to try to be someone we **think** we need to be in order to achieve who knows what. Therefore, the good news is, it is us who will learn to re-parent our own inner child and get our freedom back. We will eventually get to know and follow our blueprint.

Use my method of imagination or any method you like to achieve the altered state of the mind, but either way deep breathe and visualize yourself in the most amazing place you can imagine. Do not judge anything that comes to your mind, just let it be. There is no wrong or right. Try not to control; this place is just for you.

Once you feel at total peace, call your inner child to join you. Believe me on this, if you have not been one with your inner child for decades, she will not trust you. So this step might take time. Give her and yourself a chance. Notice how I am referring to the inner child as a separate individual than us. The truth is we are not two, but one; but for healing purposes, I will continue to do this for a while, until we can truly be one with our higher being. It will eventually happen, do not worry. This is the goal of emotional healing.

Be honest with your inner child. Tell her that she does not need to talk but to please show up. Tell her you have no clue what you are doing and that you are at least trying to get to know her. Tell her you will do anything in your power to not judge her and be nice. Remember, it is now us abandoning our inner child and for most of us this has happened for decades.

When she finally shows up, say nothing and pay close attention to the way she looks. How old is she? What is she wearing? Is she afraid? Is she happy or sad? Be as honest as you can be, tell her you do not have all the answers but that you have the best of intentions of somehow becoming friends and one with our heart again.

I believe that the age she showed up in your vision is the exact age you got stuck. The age at which we disconnected with our heart and began the auto destruction process of trying to be someone else, the one we **though**t we needed to be to find love and approval.

This is how it all began. We were born perfect. There are no perfect and imperfect babies. We were all born with a set of blueprints, which were perfect for us and our personalities. We were meant to be good at some things and bad at others, which was part of our perfection. Depending on what our parents or society said what perfection was, we began feeling good or bad, worthy or unworthy; depending how close we were to society's dictated perfection. Example: In a sport driven society, someone born to be a reader would often feel not good enough or unworthy. And all this was recorded into her subconscious mind at a young age.

Imagine a circle within a circle. We are the outer perfect circle. But we feel like the inner smaller circle, because we feel so far away from our own perception of perfection. This does not mean we are not perfect the way we are. This means we do not know at a conscious level that we were born perfect with different abilities and desires than everyone else. By our teenager years we began to compare ourselves to others and our self-esteem got worse if we did not perceive ourselves close to what society said perfection is. The way we look or do not look now came into play too. It was during our middle school years that we began patterns that made us lose ourselves even farther. We thought, "If I look a certain way others would love me. If I get invited to a certain party, I would feel better about myself. If I make it to the team, I would feel better about myself. If I get straight A's, maybe my parents will like me more, and I would feel better about myself". And when we grew, this turned into: "If I get the right job, I would be admired and I would feel better about myself". You get the picture. This is exactly how we began the hurtful process of codependency – slavery to others and circumstances outside of ourselves. This is when we learned to try to control and manipulate everyone and everything around us, making us lose ourselves even farther and more disconnected with our heart, therefore suffering more fear, anxiety and/or depression.

We are about to embark a process of self-discovery that will eventually effortlessly lead us to the truth that we are already perfect the way we are and we have always been. We will eventually encounter the truth that comes from within and set us free effortlessly. So in these first few days, listen to the way you talk to yourself (inner child) and try to be as nice and kind as possible to yourself. Be honest with your inner child and tell her this is new for you but that you now know it is not others or circumstances hurting her but us hurting ourselves. Tell her how sorry you are but had no clue at a conscious level you were doing this to her/you. Apologize!

If meditation seems too hard for you, write her a letter. Remember, do not judge, there is no right or wrong. The purpose is to make contact with your inner child.

The age of the inner child in your vision that comes to you during meditation reveals the depth of the wound. The younger, the deeper the wound. Do not be discouraged, the healing process does not have to take decades. Every new revelation of yourself is a step closer to your new life free of fear and anxiety.

The only goal at this point is for you to learn to easily imagine and visualize your inner child without trying to control any image. When you can easily see her without any overwhelming feeling and without trying to control the vision or the outcome, it would mean you are ready to move to Chapter/Activity 2. When you allow yourself to accept the vision of your most valued possession: your inner child, without any control or manipulation from your mind, then go ahead and keep reading.

I started to see the child I was and think about what that child needed. In a way I was able to re-parent myself by not stuffing old memories but by going back into them and telling that little girl that she was a good girl. I would imagine holding her and telling her that she was loved. I would tell her about parents who didn't hit or hurt, or raise their voices, which were not selfish with their love. All the while knowing that parent was me.

It was a catharsis that can't be explained. I would obsessively criticize myself for being a dumb kid and making my parent angry or knowing I was unlovable for so many things that simply were not my fault. I stopped doing that after I started re-parenting that beautiful little girl that nobody should have treated that way.

Eventually, those terrible memories stopped and I found that I loved myself.
Robin Chipman

Don't worry about losing people. Worry about losing yourself to people you won't ever please anyway.
Anonymous

2 BECOMING ONE WITH THE INNER CHILD

Did we ever lose ourselves? Everyone has their own story. We all grew up under different circumstances and different levels of craziness, or what many call dysfunctional families. But as I mentioned before, the age of your inner child that comes to mind when we stop controlling the vision, is most likely the age when we got stuck or began to lose ourselves. It was probably the very first time that we somehow felt that being ourselves was not good enough; which is the very root or beginning of our low self-esteem.

Many of us grew up without the approval of our parents. As children, we had nothing to do but pay attention and devoutly listen to every single word and action our parents said and did. We learned what they valued and didn't value and recorded that in our subconscious mind. We began to feel like we came short to what they valued. We desperately needed their approval and their love but very few received that at home. I believe this is when we must have made the unconscious decision to try and be what we **thought** they wanted us to be. This is when we began losing ourselves. This is when we became a fragmented being within and the struggle within began. The "who I am" against the "one I want to be"; a soul with two states of the mind at war with each other. This is what I call the disassociation from our own heart, the mind vs. the spirit/heart. Unfortunately many of us began to follow the lead of the mind which was loud and clear telling us who and what we needed to be in order to be loved and approved. The mind led life began producing or manifesting hell on earth or self-destruction, effortlessly producing anxiety and/or depression.

Trying to be someone we are not on a daily basis hoping to get our parent's approval formed patterns or connections in our brains becoming a way of life.

Many of us were so young we didn't even know that these patterns in our brains were forming and that later in life, these were the exact patterns that will keep us in bondage as adults; still trying to please others in order to be liked. But do not be discouraged, there is hope. We can always change our thinking and begin to form new brain patterns. I believe the easiest and fastest way to do this, is meditation, but there are many other tools we can use to reprogram our belief system about ourselves. We are definitely not powerless. We will talk about these tools in later chapters.

Before our Chapter Activity, I need for something to be very clear. We were parented in a way that left us feeling unworthy and is manifesting pain in our adult life now. This book was not written with the purpose of blaming our parents, nor even any circumstances from our past. This book will help us remember who we are and how powerful we are. The chapters ahead will teach us how to re-parent our inner child back to emotional health. We will take full responsibility for our belief system about ourselves and our brain patterns formed which resulted in the way we now treat ourselves. NOW is the only dimension that is real and eternal. As of now, we will focus on our relationship with ourselves. Later on, we will also focus on our relationships with others, which mirror our own inner world but for a while, we will only focus on our own inner parent and inner child relationship.

I have learned that the way we parent ourselves, is very similar to the way we were parented as children. If your mom was very critical of you, chances are you are your own worst critic now. If your dad only showed conditional love, chances are you are doing the same to yourself now. It is not the past or even your parents hurting you, it is now you hurting yourself. This should be good news because we do not need to change our parents in order for us to get healed. We will be focusing on changing our own inner parent in order to heal ourselves; we are the only human we can change.

For years, I did not know it was I who was making me miserable. I liked to point fingers and play victim, but none of that worked. I found myself in my forties acting like an 8 year old still trying to please and/or change my parents, others and circumstances around me.

Like most, I tried to find relationships that would fill my emotional needs. The emotional needs that were not met when I was a child but none of them worked. No one can meet our emotional needs except ourselves.

The path we are about to embark here is a path in which we will learn to meet every single one of our emotional needs and realize we are a whole person. It is the path of self-discovery and self- responsibility. It is the path of self- love and salvation; LOVE being our only savior, the love from us to ourselves.

ACTIVITY 2

Do whatever you need to achieve the altered or relaxed state of the mind. As mentioned before, I usually deep breathe and then use my imagination. This time is no different; I am asking you to imagine or visualize your inner child. By this time, this should be an easier task. I want you to focus on her face. Most likely she is very quiet and has probably zero trust towards you. Remember, you and her have been at war, probably for decades. So do not be so hard on yourself and go with the flow. It is your biggest and most valuable possession, and most likely, you did not even have a clue she even existed or was alive inside of you. Without her, you will never ever experience effortless joy and peace and feel 100% comfortable in your skin.

All I am asking today and for the next couple of days is to just be honest with her. I want you to consciously talk to her and be honest. Say what you feel or what comes to mind. Apologize if that is what you feel to do. Tell her you had no clue she was still waiting for the love and approval she never received. Take your time and do not rush this or any of these activities until you feel comfortable talking to her. Do not feel surprised if she does not say a thing. Remember, she was first abandoned by your parents, and most likely, has been abandoned by you for decades. Do not blame her for anything she did to be able to survive and/or oppress overwhelming painful feelings.

Acknowledge you both are hurting now. Tell her you had no idea it was you hurting yourself now. Be honest, tell her that you are new to this but willing to learn how to be the best friend anyone could ever have. From this moment on tell her you are going to pay attention to the way you treat her daily. Tell her you are planning on being on her side and become one with yourself and not her worse enemy.

She has been waiting for you her entire life, to come save her and receive the love and approval she needed to emotionally grow into a healthy human being. Know that she most likely will not speak for a while until she begins to experience that your actions back your words.   Enjoy and please take your time.

The True meaning of "Love your Enemy" is to learn to love thyself and thy neighbor as thyself.

Jet Magdangal

3 IT'S THE PARENT WHO NEEDS TO CHANGE

In most cases, when the child is misbehaving (whatever that means) or manifesting a behavior of self-destruction it is the mirror of the poor parenting the child has been experiencing. Unless the child is sick, it has probably developed coping mechanisms with the situation. Often, the child creates a "heart-wall" in order not to feel the overwhelming feelings of not feeling loved and/or accepted. The child in pain has two options; to oppress himself and do everything in his power to be who he thinks they are asking him to be or become a total rebellious child, in order to prove that he is ok the way he is. In both cases, the child loses itself and disassociates with his own heart creating self-destructive brain patterns that will eventually produce anxiety and depression.

The child that unconsciously chooses to rebel usually ends up making the parent mad and a lot more disapproval comes his way. Either way, the child loses. Soon the child discovers that the only way to please others is to lose himself.

Sadly, sometimes the parents that can't control and manipulate the child will go as far as to take him to therapy, hoping the therapist will be able to change the child for the better, they think. When in reality it is the parents who need therapy. Congratulations to all parents that took full responsibility and changed themselves first. No human being can give to others what they do not have. If the parent is showing and giving conditional love is because they haven't given love to themselves first. It was the parents who needed changing, never the child (at a younger age).

If this is not resolved at an early age, the child will continue to form brain patters of a coping mechanism to somehow evade pain. Coping mechanisms like a "heart-wall" helping us not to feel will have helped then, but it only worked temporary. That young man or woman will grow with self-destructing brain patterns that he or she is totally unconscious of.

Eventually, this child will turn into a teen and those coping-mechanisms like rebellion, self-denial, numbing feelings (heart-wall), trying to be perfect etc. will continue to manifest and grow. Not all teens that are self-destructive will manifest rebellion or bad behavior: some (trying to be perfect) will excel at school and look like the perfect teen. They might be the ones that are losing themselves the most and are hurting inside the most. But if the teen is not freely being himself and feeling good about himself, he will most likely develop into a miserable adult. No relationship will ever make them happy and the adult will have no idea why they are never happy.

Every child is perfect. We all came with a perfect blue-print with dreams and desires. We are all different and good at some things and bad at others. Parents, who knew this and chose to love and respect their children the way they were, gave solid good self-esteem to their children. But the more I talk to adults, the less I think this was the norm.

Most of us, by age 5, had a pretty good idea of what our parents expected from us and we gave in: in order to experience some kind of peace at home. Millions of us did not experience unconditional love growing up, creating crooked patterns in our brains. We became familiar with the gap within and for decades, we have been trying to fill the void with looks, clothes, food, no food, sex, drugs, alcohol, work, relationships, etc., and none of these worked. The only way to permanently fill our void is to meet all emotional needs that were not met as a child by our own inner parent.

As we begin this journey, remember it is a process. Meditation is going to help the process go a lot faster. The faster we learn to quiet our mind, the faster and easier it will be to uncover the truth of who we are and always have been. In case you are still having trouble with meditation, search the internet for different ways of meditation and practice.

ACTIVITY 3

Deep breathe a few times and achieve the altered state of the mind using your imagination or whatever method you like and meet your inner child again. Apologize to her for her parents that did not know how to appreciate her due to their own perceptions about themselves. Tell her it had nothing to do with her and that she is perfect the way she is and always has been. Tell her that her parents did not know this. Tell her that it has never been her responsibility to teach her parents the truth. We couldn't change our parents then, and we can't change our parents now. Tell her you are not going to use all your energy in changing them; you are going to use all your energy in trying to change yourself (the inner parent) in order to meet all her emotional needs that have not been met since birth. Tell her you are now taking full responsibility about her needs and will do anything it takes to re-learn how to self-parent and be the best you can be.

Tell her you know now it is your own preconceived ideas about her that are going to have to change and accept her as she is.

Tell your inner child repeatedly that there is nothing wrong with her and that she is and has always been good enough. Tell her you thought she was not good enough for decades, apologize.

Tell her that these preconceived ideas of what she needed to be were passed to you from past generations and you had no clue you could change that. Thank her and congratulate her for somehow surviving all these years even after being oppressed for decades. Ask for an opportunity to change and the opportunity to self-heal.

Tell her it is you and your thinking that needs to change now, never her. She is and has always been the most amazing manifestation on the planet. We all are, period!

Even relatively "good" parents have expectations, and when the toddler fails to please his parents, it feels to him that he is falling short, not good enough. Then add in religion telling us we are all sinners and need to be saved. By the time we come to understand that we are perfect, we've got a lot of crap buried in our unconscious mind. It really takes work for most of us to be true to ourselves, which of course includes loving ourselves.

Brenda Bender

A lot of parents will do anything for their kids, except let them be themselves."

Banksy

4 THE BACKWARD ROLES

When a child is born, he is pretty much helpless. He can't do anything for himself. All he could do was cry and ask for help. For most of us, we all had good parenting in the physical department; our diapers were changed and we were fed regularly. My heart goes out to all those who their physical needs were not met.

I believe there is a multitude of reasons and preconceived ideas why parents have children. Some may just found themselves having sex and got pregnant. Many more planned it. But how many parents had children for the mere purpose of loving the child? I do not know. How many had children due to the preconceived idea that one has to have a family to be happy? How many parents had children in hopes their own kids will fill the emotional void they had inside and meet their needs? The point I am trying to make is that many children came into this world as a means of making the parents happy and so much was expected of them and were treated as possessions.

While the kid can be controlled, it is easy for the child to meet the emotional needs of the parent, but surprise, surprise: once the kid begins to grow, he or she has an opinion of his own and he can't be controlled that easily. The truth is, the child is not an extension of the parent. The child is a complete whole individual separate from the parent. The child has his own temper, his own soul, his own set of prints that are only known to him. The child has his own deep desires and abilities. Most parents failed to honor who the child was and began to control and manipulate their children into being what they **thought** he needed to be, for his own good, they **thought**. All this is unconsciously done and they deeply believe they are loving and helping educate/raise the child. But the fact is that not respecting the child for who he is, is child abuse, whether they know it or not.

Different children react in different ways. Many rebel even more, with hopes that their parents would finally see their worth and flourish being who they are. Many others give in hoping of receiving some sort of love and approval and do not rock the boat of anger at home.

The truth is that parents were supposed to be the biggest fans of their children and not their biggest oppressors and manipulators. Parents are the gardeners of the garden. As gardeners, aren't we supposed to trust the seeds knowing what they are doing in order to become the plant they were supposed to be? Aren't the gardeners only in charge of watering and taking care of the garden? Or can the gardener tell the plant how to be and how to grow into what the gardener **thinks** the plant should be? My point is, few of us grew up feeling respected and honored for who we are.

My true self has been suffocated by the voice of one saying that I must do, be, look, act, etc. a certain way; and if I don't, I will suffer. But the true me is suffering behind the mask. Edie Chill

I believe we all experienced conditional love at different levels. It is about time that those roles are reversed. We did not come to earth to fill the emotional needs of our parents. We came here to flourish and be happy as we freely manifest our true self. It is not our parents or our past hurting us now, it is us hurting ourselves now. Let's take full responsibility and begin meeting our needs by parenting and gardening our garden, our soul.

Pay attention to how you parent yourself. Are you supportive and your own best friend? Or are you your biggest worst enemy? In this Activity, we will reverse the role of the parent and child.

FALLING IN LOVE WITH YOURSELF

We are going to stop being the child of our physical parents and release them from their job. We are going to stop trying to please them and trying to get their approval.

We are going to become our own parents and give to ourselves the perfect parenting we needed and should have received decades ago. For the very first time, we are going to allow the child to lead and teach/show us who he is and was meant to be. Trust that evidently, he knows better. From today on we would only be the gardener of our own child and we will patiently listen on how he wants to be helped.

ACTIVITY 4

Do whatever it takes to reach the altered state of the mind with the help of deep breathing and imagination. Invite your inner child and wait for him to show up. Apologize for his well-intentioned parents that did not know he knew better and that it was totally ok the way he was. Apologize for the parents not knowing that the only way for him to be happy was to allow him to be who he was.

Explain that you will take over as of today and that his actual physical parents are now released of their job. Explain that you still have no idea how you are going to do this, but willing to learn to quiet the controlling mind in order to listen to his still small voice. Acknowledge that you know he knows better in every situation. Tell him you are planning on coming to him and listen to what he has to say, as he knows better in all circumstances, and show you the path of emotional healing.

Be completely honest, tell him you are still struggling with control and not knowing how he really is and that you are little afraid to let go. You have never done this before.

Tell him you are planning on letting go of the control and setting him free and that it is scary for you. We have no idea what kinds of feelings are going to show up. Be honest, and tell him you are planning on trying and will somehow allow him to lead.

For many of us this is a tough thing to do. To set our own inner child free is beyond scary. We have controlled him to the most minimum of details. I used to believe (preconceived ideas from religion) that I was a sinner at heart. I deeply believed that if I set myself free to do as I pleased; I was going to go into a sin stampede. I had no more options but to set myself free, anxiety was killing me inside. I let go one step at a time, one hour at a time, one afternoon at a time. To my surprise, after a week and a lot of setbacks, I began noticing that all I desired to do was to enjoy life and love. I did not go after sex and drugs. I did not desire to be selfish. All I deeply desired was to love and be loved. I discovered by a deep experience I was not a sinner after all. It was the first time I saw myself as pure and beautiful. I experientially found out that only love came from my inside inner child. It was very eye opening for me; I finally consciously knew that I was good at heart.

I believe that if I have never had the courage to set my inner child free I would still believe I was not good at all and I would still be manifesting hell on earth around me and continued on with self-destructive patterns. I began with very little baby steps. If I was invited to a social event; I asked her if she wanted to go. I did as it led me. Soon I began to experience joy everywhere I went or did not go. I discovered that my inner child was trustable and she really knew better what was best for me. This was the very beginning of me and my inner child becoming one and the same, and on the same team. Baby Steps!

Please stay here as long as you need, this step can take weeks and it is totally ok. There is lots more work to do on the following chapters; we will learn how to be assertive and set healthy boundaries, so take your time.

5 THE FEAR OF BEING SELFISH

We all have preconceived ideas of what "being selfish" is. The most common one is that "being selfish" is bad and produces a life of misery to all those around us. I happen to believe that "selfishness" has a huge purpose in the growth of all individuals. It is good, normal and necessary in the life of a child to achieve healthy maturity. Children are in the process of finding who they are. As they experience selfishness, they will develop a healthy self-esteem and a sense of power and wholeness. This would help them know that they are as important as everyone else. The problem here is that most parents do not know that this is a normal and a necessary phase. So good intentioned parents try to educate and change the child into being good and giving. The parent begins to say things like this, "Now be a good boy and share your toys." Do you see all that this well intentioned comment implies? Yes, it implies, "If you do not feel like sharing, you must be a bad boy." This is what the child deeply listens to and is recorded in his subconscious mind reinforcing the lie he is no good. A wiser parent should have said something like, "Visitors are coming today, go ahead and hide all the toys you do not want to share and leave all others where they can be seen and shared." This totally implies, I respect your feelings and you are good.

The healthy/selfish child should have learned that he is as worthy as everyone else and that all feelings that come from within are to be respected and honored and that there is no need to put himself last: "Love others as yourself".

After the phase of selfishness is over and has done the

job, the child would have effortlessly moved into a new phase, where it should have discovered on its own that playing alone is not always fun. He, out of love, not guilt and shame, effortlessly would have moved on into healthy sharing.

Most of us grew up under the blanket of "being selfish is a horrible sin" and never achieved a healthy sense of power and wholeness. We began to put others first, out of duty and not love or because it made us feel a little better about ourselves. This produced two kinds of adults, the narcissist (it is all about me) or the giver (walk all over me) adults.

I believe that for all of us that were raised under this mindset would need to go into a healthy phase of selfishness to achieve a healthy sense of wholeness. "Put yourself first for a while and see what happens, let go!"

Many of us that have put ourselves last and abandoned ourselves on a daily basis for decades will have to go through the "selfish process" we missed and put ourselves first (in every area of our lives) for a while (at least a year or two) or as long as it takes, to mature - until we desire to put everyone (including ourselves) as equals.

Afraid others won't like you if you put yourself first?
The ones that like you for who you are, won't leave. The ones that can't use you anymore will disappear quickly and guess what? That is perfectly ok. The feeling that you matter, is unbelievably healing. Every human being has to be selfish at some point in their lives, is a part of healthy growing up.

It is not until we radically love ourselves (our inner child) that we will be able to radically love others. At the same level we love ourselves, is the same level we truly love (don't need and use) others.

I do not think it is selfish to take care of ourselves, it is necessary. Sometimes, when people take care of themselves first are labeled as "selfish" and it will be used by others to try to control, and manipulate them back to their original mentality of the door mat. In reality, taking care of ourselves, learning to set healthy boundaries and being assertive is necessary to experience and re-record our subconscious mind with the truth that we matter and are worthy, just as everyone else is.

ACTIVITY 5

Close your eyes, deep breathe and achieve the altered state of the mind. Imagine a situation of something you always do but hate doing to either please others or because we are afraid others won't like you when you say "no".

Now go ahead and imagine the same scenario, but you being totally able and at peace replying, "no" to that person or group of persons. Imagine yourself being totally assertive and saying, "I am sorry, I can't do or go with you this time." and do not give any further explanations.

Check on your feelings, was this easy or hard to imagine? Talk to your inner child and assure her, it is totally ok to put herself first. Explain that this should have been done long ago, better late than ever anyway. Explain this is what emotionally healthy people do and should have been the norm. Focus on her/your feelings; assure her this is new to you and it will get easier with time.

Practice this exercise again and again until you feel at peace and know it is ok to honor your own feelings and that you matter. Imagine this same situation with different people and different sets of circumstances until you feel comfortable being assertive and setting healthy boundaries.

This exercise will probably take a little longer until we deeply know that we and our feelings matter. Once you feel a little more comfortable, go ahead and practice in front of a mirror. Practice how to answer, "Let me think about it." Then practice a comeback with, "I am sorry but I do not think I can go this time."

FALLING IN LOVE WITH YOURSELF

Confrontation is hard for almost everyone, so do not be so hard on yourself and begin to say "no" on a text, then on the phone, until you get so good at this that you can easily say "no" face to face without feeling guilty. You matter.

After a lifetime of suppressing my feelings I began to face them and began to heal. It has been painful and sad but I am so grateful for the peace that I am beginning to experience. The ability to love myself continues to expand and embrace all the parts of me that I have tried to push away.
Barbara

The most wonderful moment in a woman's life is when she realizes she can do whatever she wants, and she does not owe anyone an explanation and she doesn't need anyone's permission. She is just living and that is beautiful.
Anonymous

6 WHO SAID YOU WERE NAKED?

Do we know who we are? Or do we **think** we know who we are due to all preconceived ideas passed to us from generations? Without all preconceived ideas, who are we? If the truth sets us free and we are not experiencing effortless freedom and peace, we for sure do not know the truth about who we are.

Are we a mere human with a god out there? How is it working? Is he helping any? Is he healing sick children, is he feeding the hungry, is he stopping human trafficking, is he stopping abuse, is he healing all good people from cancer? While many will argue with me that he provides and knows better, I insist: Where is he?

Have you ever closed your eyes and received higher truth within that set you free in an instant (twinkle of an eye)? Have you ever asked within yourself about something that troubles you and all of a sudden you hear the answer that makes it all make sense? Have you ever listened to a still small voice inside of you that set you back in the right path? Have you ever had an intuition and it turned out true? Have you ever had a dream that gave you higher truth or information that helped with your struggles?

Where is this higher truth coming from and how come we were not taught how to retrieve this information from our own within? Why are so many afraid of meditation? Didn't the bible say over and over again that Jesus separated himself to meditate?

The most common teaching in western countries is that there is a god out there, perfect and loving, but he somehow only helps when enough people ask or when he feels it is good for us. The common excuse is "his ways are higher than ours". What kind of an excuse is this? In the eastern countries meditation is taught at an early age. Didn't Jesus say, "The kingdom is within"? So why are we still looking for a god out there?

Could it be that Jesus, Buddha and others are symbols of our own true self? Could it be that we are not mere humans but spirit in flesh? Why are we not taught on how to achieve a spirit/heart led life instead of a mind/carnal one?

It all began for me in 2012 when I learned I was one with god, not two: therefore god in the flesh. I know this is a hard pill to swallow for many that were raised in fundamental Christianity. I just don't buy anymore the theory of, "a god out there that finds good parking spots and forgets to feed dying kids in Africa". We are the only manifestation (Universe) of god that we will ever have and if we do not feed those kids in Africa, then god won't. Yes, one spirit, manifested in one humanity.

This humongous shift in my thinking has put back all responsibility on me and ended my victim mentality within a flash. This shift in thinking is now effortlessly producing heaven on earth in my life. If I wanted a different kind of life, it was me and only me who needed to make the changes. No one else could. I stopped wanting others to change, I stopped controlling and manipulating people and circumstances and I began pointing at me. I stopped being co-dependent to a non-existent daddy in heaven that refused to help me when I begged, fasted, and prayed. It was all up to me and that was good news. I could not change a god out there, but I could certainly change me.

I understood I was 100% responsible for the kind of life I had and that the only person I could change was me. I began meeting all my emotional needs. I began loving and accepting myself. It finally felt that god loved me, because I began loving myself for the first time in my life.

I began to experience that I was whole. I and god are

one: not two. Isn't this what Jesus tried to model? Didn't he say, "When you see me, you see the father"? When Jesus asked why he was being stoned, didn't the Pharisees answered, "We do not stone you because of your miracles, we stone you because you, a mere man, makes yourself god"? Doesn't the bible say, "As he is, so are we in this world"?

If you desire a deeper understanding of how I came to believe I was one with god and not two, supported with scripture from the book of John please read my book "Oneness" written after a revelation I received within from spirit in 2012.

God has no beginning and no end, and is eternal. He is not a he or a she and it is not independent of you. God is everything you see and don't see. (Quantum Physics) So when I say, "god is us", I am not talking about a separate person or individual, I am talking about the omnipresent eternal energy.

Once you think of god as a person, it implies you are a separate entity (two and not one) and immediately think of yourself as an inferior and limited human being – a mere powerless human. As we worship a perfect god out there we are reinforcing the lie of separation that led to universal low self-esteem. As we believed the lie of separation, we manifested failure reinforcing the lie even farther that kept us in bondage.

I happen to believe that any religion, sect, guru or teacher that does not point back at you, at your own divine power and responsibility is indeed a lie that will keep you in bondage.

It is ok if you struggle with this new way of thinking. It took me a while to realize I was not a "good for nothing sinner" they said I was. One thing I know for sure – we manifest what we deeply believe. We will never be able to accept ourselves until we deeply know we are not sinners, good for nothing. We are divine in flesh and we can effortlessly manifest that at the same level that we consciously know and believe it.

ACTIVITY 6

The amount of time you spend in this chapter is up to you. I know I will lose many and of those many, some will come back when the lesson is learned. I invite you to meditate and ask within. I invite you to read my book "Oneness" and trust your heart and only your heart. This is nothing but good news but many struggle getting rid of the preconceived ideas passed to us from generations. Is this too good to be true? Yes, it is.

Close your eyes and achieve the altered state of the mind, and invite your inner child to show up. Ask him for forgiveness and explain how you were led to believe he was a sinner good for nothing. Tell him that somehow we are going to get our own power back and begin to change our life for the better. Tell him that you have plans of ending the victim mentality that was instilled in him/you as a child. Hug him big.

When did I realize god is not a person out there? I realized it when I read the very first page, "Let US make man in OUR image". That is when I realized what it meant. That shifted my whole existence. Whichever way you look at it...it says, US! That made me think twice.

Arius Alexander King

Who said you were naked and a mere man? You are divinity in flesh.

7 MANIFESTING HEAVEN ON EARTH

How exactly do we achieve a spirit-led life that effortlessly manifests heaven on earth vs. a mind-led life that is effortlessly manifesting hell on earth? There is no other way around it, we all manifest what we deeply believe and was recorded in our subconscious mind. If we deeply believe we are a loser, no matter how hard we try and work, we will always lose at anything we attempt. If we do not ever question our belief system just for the simple reason that it was passed on to us by generations and is what most around us believe, we are living unconsciously or what many call, in a sleep state.

But if we begin questioning our own belief system for the simple reason that our life is actually not working and are tired of living with anxiety and depression, we will begin to wake up and live consciously. We will begin to make conscious decisions that match our new belief system and begin manifesting a different life.

In my last book, "Levels of Awakening" I went through big lengths explaining about our two mind hemispheres and how the marriage the bible talks about, refers to the carnal mind and the submission to the spirit mind. "Woman, submit to your husband."- meaning Mary (the flesh) submit to your father (the spirit) and produce the Christ, or the mind of Christ: a carnal mind submitted to the spirit mind producing fruit; "the fruit of the spirit-joy, peace, love, etc."

For all of you who did not grow up under fundamentalism I am going to make it even simpler. Our mind (thinking) needs to submit to our spirit (heart). Many call our carnal mind, "the ego" and continuously repeat that we need to kill the ego. In my opinion, there is absolutely nothing wrong with me that needs to be killed. The only thing that needs to be killed is my wrong thinking produced by a lie I somehow still believe and is still manifesting hell on earth. Other than that, nothing in me needs to be killed. Our mind is our helper and is 100% necessary to live on earth. Our mind is the one in charge of manifesting our divinity on earth.

The problem began when we were not taught to meditate and to reach inside of us for higher truth. The problem continued when no one modelled a spirit-led life for us. Due to emotional pain, the problem got even bigger when we built a heart-wall around our heart as a coping mechanism for pain and did all in our power to avoid feeling. Little by little we formed patterns in our brains of how to live guided by the mind in its entirety and not our heart. Example, "I should look this way, act this way, feel this way, … should, should, should…instead of asking ourselves, "How do I feel today, why do I feel this way, and what do you feel about this decision? etc."

Many of us grew up believing there was nothing good in us, so how were we supposed to trust our own feelings and internal guide?

What I will explain here: many call, "to be centered", but it is nothing more than being in contact with your inner child (heart) at all times for all decisions. Followed by learning to be assertive and to act accordingly. It will take time and lots of practice but eventually: this new way of thinking and feeling will become the new way of living.

Some of us even forgot how to feel and the only time we cry is during a sad movie, we find it very hard to get in touch with our feelings again. My suggestion here is to pay close attention to our peace level. Our loss of peace needs to become our best helper or guide now, it is our red flag. Every time I lose my peace and fear/anxiety is felt, I just know I have disconnected with my heart and I am acting according to my thinking and not my feelings. I then know it is time to meditate. I have become so good at this that it only takes 2-3 deep breaths and I am right there: at the altered state of the mind. Once I am there, I ask within, "Why do I feel this way, what am I doing wrong, what is the lie buried deep in my belief system that is manifesting this anxiety?"

The answer to each of those questions comes to me as a thought or idea. Although it has come in words but that is not "the normal" for me. How do I know that I heard right? The thought or idea comes with an unexplainable overwhelming peace and sense of freedom in that area.

For me, this happens when somehow I am losing contact with my heart and trying to please others unconsciously. Usually the thought will be something like this, "And why do you even want them to like you?" Nothing else needs to be said. This brings me to the lie that I might be inferior to others, because of this and that.

I then consciously focus back in the truth that sets me free: "I am whole, I am ok, and I'm never inferior. And whether they like me or not is up to them. I can definitely survive if they do not like me." This inner process can happen in a few minutes and I go back to experiencing total peace.

Another way I tend to get my peace back is by asking about the facts (not perceptions) about the situation. Example: When someone makes me feel inferior and I lose my peace and my cool. I quiet myself as soon as possible and I ask myself, "What are the facts about this situation?" This comes to mind, "The truth/fact is: no one can make me feel inferior. Therefore it is me and my preconceived ideas that are making me feel inferior. The fact is that every human being is equally valuable". This is usually enough to bring my peace back.

Then I know that this is the perfect time for me to meditate on my preconceived ideas about my value in reference to others and get rid of the lies once and for all.

FALLING IN LOVE WITH YOURSELF

ACTIVITY 7

This time I want you to close your eyes and meditate with these questions in mind. Write down all the questions if this is easier for you, then be as honest as possible and answer them in that piece of paper. The purpose of this exercise is to go deep into your belief system and find out a few lies that are keeping you in bondage and fear.

What do you think about rich people, poor people, sick people, children, fat people, thin people, short people, and tall people? What do you think about yourself? Does your worth change depending on how much money you have? How you look? What job you have? What car you drive and the size of your dress?

Do you feel inferior when you interact with certain people? Describe them. How do you feel when you are around successful people? (Whatever that means depending on your preconceived ideas). What makes them better or worse? Says who? Who told you, you were naked and a mere human? Who told you, you were not good enough? At what age? Why? Is that a fact or just a preconceived idea passed on to your from generations? What is the truth about you? Are you still trying to be perfect? What does "perfect" mean to you? Says who?

We all grew up with different perceptions but the truth that will set you free -once and for all- is that every human being is equally valuable: independently from looks and circumstances. What makes the difference is what every individual believes to be true about himself. Remember, we all manifest what we deeply believe.

Take your time, a week or two, discerning your belief system about yourself in relationship or in comparison to others. Question it all? Ask all the whys? Ask yourself why you believe a certain way; is it a fact or just a theology, or preconceived idea passed on to you and recorded in your subconscious mind?

Who said skinny people are better than fat people? Are they really happier? What is the fact, the truth? What makes us valuable? Take your time.

The happier individuals I know are the ones that accept themselves the way they are today. They love themselves unconditionally, meaning without judgment. Those are the ones that don't spend their time judging themselves and others. This is good news: set yourself free from all lies and preconceived ideas that are not aligned with the higher truth that every human being is valuable as they are and where they are in their journey.

8 WHAT IS PERFECTIONISM?

Nothing has hurt me more than the thought of perfection. Nothing gave me more low self-esteem than believing in a perfect god "out there". The lie of separation (theology of dualism: me and god are two) had me deeply believing that he was good and I was not. Sadly, the worshipping and the praying for more of him and less of me deeply reinforced the lie, manifesting in more and more low self-esteem and a life of self-destruction and defeat.

Who gets to say what "perfect" is anyway? What is perfection? This is what Wikipedia has to say about perfection: Perfection is a state, variously, of completeness, flawlessness, or supreme excellence.

Who exactly can meet those requirements? No one, except our preconceived idea of a perfect god out there. That's it, no one else. But, is this god even real? When I read the bible I soon found out that god ordered to kill many in the old testament . . . was that perfection?

God ordering to kill an entire town and to keep the virgins as sex slaves, is that perfection? (Numbers 31:17) Certainly not to me. So who in the world is perfect? The answer is: all of us, only we fail to know this at a conscious level. Let me explain my train of thought. The only incredible perfect entity is our spirit. Yes, there is only one spirit and it is manifested in the universe through one humanity. So how come the universe does not manifest perfection?

We all can easily see that we do not live in a perfect universe. Just yesterday there was a storm at our place that destroyed a bird house with little baby birds in it. The birds were not ready to fly and yes, you guessed it, raccoons ate them at night.

Where is this perfect god that is supposed to protect birds and humans? What is this evil we see in this world? The spirit is, always has been and always will be perfect love. A utopia kind of thing. The more we live led by the spirit, the more we consciously know the higher truth, the more we will manifest heaven on earth. No way around it, we manifest what we deeply believe, not what we want.

So what is all this evil we see in this world? It is nothing more than the full manifestation of universal consciousness (what most believe). So if the entire world continues to believe in the power of demonic forces, guess what will continue to manifest and see? Yes, demonic forces. But where is the devil? Where is god? Is it even possible that heaven and earth are not places but states of our one mind now? It is us who manifest heaven (or hell) on earth now, depending on our belief system. The understanding of this helped me tremendously.

Can I be perfect? Sure I can, when I am totally dead and do not have a flesh mind, ha! But I can tell you this, the more I live led by my spirit, the more my life manifests perfection/divinity. The more I believe that the entire humanity is one humanity and is perfect love (even though I do not see this with my two eyes, I see it with my eye of the spirit/heart) the more I live in heaven on earth.

What happens when I meet an individual that is self-destructing, is that person perfect? He is, only he still does not know this at a conscious level. Jesus did not see the prostitute, he saw her pure heart. When are we going to stop judging everything and everyone as good and evil? Evil is not reality. Our only reality is spirit and is perfect love. But it will not be manifested until we totally believe we are who we are: spirit in flesh.

Guess "when" are you going to be able to love others unconditionally (the love that heals: lack of judgment)? Bingo, when you stop judging yourself as good or bad,

SETTING MYSELF FREE FROM MY OWN MIND.

good or evil.

Do not judge others if you do not want to be judged. I say, do not judge yourself, so you stop judging others. Just this morning I saw a meme shared by a good christian friend of mine on Facebook, making fun of Michelle Obama's outfit in comparison to Melania Trump's outfit. It made me so sad: a christian judging and making fun of someone's outfit? Her post does not talk about Michelle or even her outfit; it talks loud and clear about how judgmental most christians are, how comfortable we have become in judging others to the point of sharing it on Facebook and publicly laughing about it. When are we going to be the light, as Jesus said, and begin loving others without judgment? I will tell you when: when we stop judging ourselves.

The goal is not to be perfect, whatever that means. Remember, perfection is in the hands of the beholder or the observer. What is perfect music? Well, that depends in what we know about music and our likes and dislikes. So a perfect song for me can be a horrible song for you, right? So perfection is not even real, or is it?

I believe it is, just not the way it was understood in my mind. We see perfection every single day. We see many, many things going well on a daily basis, but our minds were trained to focus on the things that go wrong instead. Just looking at my backyard right now I see the other three birdhouses that did not fall with the storm. I see my backyard full of birds. I see trees and flowers. I see perfection, the spirit of god. I see me, I see you, and I see the life I have now. Is it perfect? Well it depends.

I have chosen to believe that I am perfectly manifesting my own belief system. I have chosen to be happy with where, who I am and what I have today.

Perfection is to know that, as time passes, we continue to be in contact with our spirit and discover more and more truth about who humanity is. The closer I get to consciously knowing higher truth, the closer I will get to

SETTING MYSELF FREE FROM MY OWN MIND.

manifesting heaven (perfect love and peace) on earth.
This will take me to our next chapter --our world reflects our inner belief system. Hang on. Before we move on, let us do our activity.

ACTIVITY 8

For this activity I want you to meditate on what you read today. What is perfection to you? Have you been trying to be perfect your entire life? What for? So others may like you? Well let me tell you: people are manifesting their and your self-esteem simultaneously. People will not like you if you do not like yourself and/or if they do not like themselves. And there is nothing we can do about this. Now this should set us free.

Please meditate on this. Bring your inner child and hug her. Is she perfect to you, you bet she is. When was the last time she heard that she already is perfect just the way she is? Are you still judging her for her feelings, desires and choices? Are you still judging yourself as good or/and evil? Be honest. If so, apologize.

It does not have to be perfect to be good. We will not be set free until our self-esteem solely comes from just being in the present moment. Not how we look, or what we have, our relationships or anything we do. Just be. Repeat this to yourself, "I am good just because I am here right now breathing".

I believe I experienced the last judgment in 2012. That was the last time I unconsciously judged myself.

A phrase I tell myself that helps me on a daily basis is this. After experiencing the tiniest form of fear or anxiety I tell myself: "Just do your best and see what happens". This takes the pressure off of me and all kinds of expectations too. This works like a charm. Apply this for the next week or two and see how your anxiety levels change.

SETTING MYSELF FREE FROM MY OWN MIND.

9 OUR LIFE MIRRORS OUR OWN BELIEF SYSTEM

In this chapter we are going to focus on our relationships . . . so hang on.

About time we stop blaming others and circumstances for our life. It is our belief system that is being manifested on a daily basis. Are you still trying to change others so that they meet your needs and love you in a certain way? Well, that totally shows that you do not love yourself. Are you in an abusive relationship? That shows you are abusing yourself and you might not love yourself and believe that you are worthy of respect. "Are you respecting yourself?" would be the question to ask yourself.

It has been a very long process for me and a painful one too. You are not here to "hear" about me, so I will try to keep it short. I grew up in a house where love and approval were not given to me. At least not in the way I wanted or needed it. It was not until my forties that I realized my mom was not going to approve of me no matter what I did or did not do. By that time I was already married to a man who repeated my story.

I finally left the marriage: not because of the cheating and disrespect, done to me. I left because the internal pain was unbearable, I did not feel loved by him. The cheating was just the perfect kick in the back I needed to force me to leave.

A few months after moving to another house and my children watching me cry daily, my oldest daughter said something to me that clicked inside of me. She said, "Why do you even want a man like this in your life?" Just, right

SETTING MYSELF FREE FROM MY OWN MIND.

there she empowered me. I am not the victim here and it is me who does not want this in my life. I do not know exactly if I was ready to hear this or what happened, but I did not cry a day after that.

It was a bloody divorce and a great attempt at destroying me but it made me stronger instead. I totally believe that divorces sometimes are good and necessary. I do not feel guilty about it; I only wish we would have done it in a healthier way in order to not hurt the children. My ex took me to court repeatedly and accused me of things I have never heard before. You name it, from abandoning my children and only wanting money, to mental health. After a few years of this, I left town. The more I defended myself, the louder the disrespect got, not only from him but also from some of my children. Some of my children went from love to hate and disrespect within a few months. They left me, packed their stuff behind my back and left my house, making sure I knew they did not want to live with me. Two of my five kids stood up for me and continued to love and respect me. The other three stopped all kind of communication with me. Why am I sharing this here? Because this painful situation is what gave me the opportunity to grow.

All my important relationships in my life perfectly modelled my own low self-esteem. I wanted my parents to love me while growing up. Then I wanted my ex to love me for two decades. Now I found myself devastated, wanting my children to love me. Isn't this repetitive? Same story, different people? Isn't it true that the lesson will continue to repeat itself until we learn? It sure did in my case. Here I was, still wanting my significant others to love me. Did they love me? Sure they did. My parents loved me the best way they could and knew. My ex loved me in so many ways. My children loved me, I knew that. We had an amazing relationship before the divorce.

The lesson here is that it is me who is responsible for meeting my emotional needs and not anyone else. After

SETTING MYSELF FREE FROM MY OWN MIND.

crying myself to sleep countless nights, due to some of my children not talking to me for years, I decided it was me who needed to change. At Christmas, about two or three years ago, I cried for three days straight, until I finally said, "This is it. I cannot spend my life crying." I decided that I was going to have to learn to be happy with what I had. I now had an amazing husband who loved me and I had two children that loved me too. So I had two options, begin taking antidepressants or start to be happy with myself and enjoy those who loved me. I chose option two and began enjoying life again. I was not enjoying my two kids, because I spent my days thinking of the three I wanted to love me.

My biggest lesson was this: my goal was not for my children to come back and make me whole. My goal was that I was OK whether they came back or not. I was whole with or without children, my higher being said so and I believed. After letting go, my life became happy again.

A few years after that two more of my kids began having a relationship with me. I have never been so happy in my life. That leaves me with only one child still not talking to me up to this day. I would love for him to come back and have a relationship with me, but I am whole and OK, no matter what. See the difference? I want him to come back; I do not need him to come back. And actually my goal now is not that they love me; my goal is that they all learn how amazing they are and love and respect themselves. My biggest desire is that they find effortless love and peace within.

And here I am: codependent no more. I wrote this not to blame anyone. I take full responsibility, not for my younger years but for all my adult years. It is me who sets the stage for the respect I expect from others because of the own respect I give to myself. My feelings matter. I matter. My relationships matter. These have been the three harder lessons that I have endured and overcame, or should I say, "One repetitive lesson"?

SETTING MYSELF FREE FROM MY OWN MIND.

My biggest puzzle is now solved. I do not need anyone to love me, and it is me who does not want disrespectful relationships in my life. Not now, not ever.

My now new-found love for myself is now manifesting healthy relationships only. It is a choice and it was me who changed it. No, I can't change people, but I can always change my own belief system. I did.

The rapture happened to me in 2012, when I was awakened to higher dimensions of truth about myself. I sure did leave many behind, including members of my family. I went to heaven on earth, leaving many behind in their hell on earth and in hopes they find and create their own heaven on earth as they discover higher truth about themselves.

ACTIVITY 9

Meditate on what repetitive lessons the universe is giving you. Meditate and why you are not solving them. Are you still in the victim mentality and think you do not have options? What are your options? Can you go back to school? Can you leave the abuser? Can you get a new job? Can you attend a seminar about learning to meditate? Can you begin loving yourself? Can you begin respecting yourself?

Describe your relationships? What kind of relationships do you have? On a 0-10 scale, how good are they? Just know that if you do not change a thing, nothing will change. Our relationships and circumstances perfectly model our belief system about ourselves. If we do not start deeply believing we deserve better, we will never get better, because we will continue to sabotage ourselves.

You will not get emotionally healed until you know this. The disrespect done to you is actually you disrespecting yourself.

10 FULLY ACCEPTANCE OF OUR BODIES

We cannot go to the next level of healing until we accept our present physical aspect. I do not know if there is a wrong or right way to learn to love, approve and accept our bodies. Just as we needed emotional love and acceptance, our physical existence needs it too. We need to not fight, but be friends with the way we look. Who defines pretty? Who defines what the perfect weight is for us? It's all about perception, again.

So my take here is for us to love ourselves with the physical aspect that we have now, today. Do we need to exercise more and eat better? Maybe. But try not to be your worst enemy and see where you are as a result of what was put in your subconscious mind and also the way we developed eating/exercise patterns as children.

Yes, maybe we need to exercise more and eat better, but are you holding your love to you because of the way you look? How would you treat your best friend if she was not at her best now? Would you encourage her or criticize her? Go ahead and be honest. We are usually super nice to others but very mean to ourselves. It is what it is today and I am not waiting to be at my best to begin loving this body, period. Decide this today and see what happens.

When was the last time you thanked your heart for working properly? What if we changed our thinking from being dis-grateful to being grateful? How about we thank our legs? These are the only two legs we will have for the rest of our lives, so be nice to them.

It has been proven that plants react to nice words and sounds. Imagine if the cells in your body are listening to

SETTING MYSELF FREE FROM MY OWN MIND.

your voice 24/7 and nothing respectful comes from you? Imagine what would happen if your cells receive nothing but love from you? Imagine that! Wouldn't that be a huge part on our healing process, not only emotionally but physically too? How about encouraging words instead of condemnation to our own bodies and cells? Lots to think about here.

Take care of your body the best you can today. Do not get upset for setbacks. Most of us eat or don't eat due to emotional pain, it is ok. Do not be hard on yourself, we are working on it.

ACTIVITY 10

I want you to do the same thing you have been doing for a while now and go spend some time with your inner child. Tell her whatever it is you are feeling now, in regards to her looks and body. Apologize if you need to. It is all ok. Tell her you have good intentions of not being so hard and begin to be kind in relationship to her physical aspect. Do this as long as it takes to realize how much you continue to hurt her feelings on a daily basis and know this has to change.

I also want to do a separate meditation in which you are to concentrate in every part of your body. I usually begin at the top and go down, but there is no right or wrong way to meditate. I inhale air and see it as healing light and I exhale and see that as low vibration energy (disease) leaving my body. I deep breathe as many times I need to be able to relax my body and reach the altered state of the mind. I am going to ask you to relax from top to bottom, beginning with your face, and chin and then your shoulders; until you end up with your toes. This time not only ask that part of your body to relax but also be grateful for that body part. Thank your neck, your arms, hands, etc.

SETTING MYSELF FREE FROM MY OWN MIND.

After that, I want you to focus on your insides. Focus on every mayor system or organs and thank them for working the best they can. Then talk to your cells and thank them for doing a magnificent job. I want you to end with seeing the light go over all of your body physically healing whatever needs to be healed. As you exhale, see all kind of disease leaving your body. Imagine if we do this once a day for a month? What do you think would happen to your body and health?

    Find some guided meditations or create your own that helps you to accept your body. Stop apologizing for the way you look. Start embracing your body. If your way of eating is not working, find one that suits you. Remember, baby steps. Do not be so hard on yourself. I do not think that radical diets work. We need to change from the inside out. If you know that seven sodas a day is not good; start with only drinking two a day for a week, and go from there. Baby steps into a new lifestyle is what has worked for me.

SETTING MYSELF FREE FROM MY OWN MIND.

11 CHILDHOOD – ELEMENTARY YEARS

We cannot move to healing our middle school years until something is clear and healed. You need to spend as much time as you need healing your childhood and elementary years. It is all up to you. We are getting closer to the end of this section in this book.

I want you to "test the waters" before you move on with healing your inner young teen. Childhood was about our basic needs being met. I am talking about physical and emotional needs like food, safety, love, approval and a healthy feeling of belonging. If you are not meeting all these needs for yourself now, do not move on and stay here a little longer. I am not talking about perfection. Do you feel loved by you most of the time? Do your actions and words back this up?

Or are you still putting yourself in circumstances where you do not think you matter and you feel unsafe? Are you pleasing others to be liked? Look at your life. Observe your life from the past seven days. Where are you on the self-love department, 0 to 10? Are you making yourself feel safe? Has your inner child begun to trust you? Because you can say the right words all you want; your inner child will not trust you until he sees some actions backing up your words. You decide.

ACTIVITY 11

I just want you to spend time with yourself and decide

SETTING MYSELF FREE FROM MY OWN MIND.

if you are ready to move on to begin healing your young teen. If you feel you are, go ahead and do the utopia meditation for your inner child in the next chapter. Enjoy!

SETTING MYSELF FREE FROM MY OWN MIND.

12 UTOPIA MEDITATION
AGES 0-7/ CHILDHOOD

Root chakra – grounding struggles

If we were lucky enough to start this life as babies who felt loved, desired and approved we will most likely be very well grounded and have a strong sense of loving life, rarely feel depressed and have lots of energy. But if we, as children, were rarely touched, felt unloved and felt like we were not good enough, or nothing we did got the approval of our caregivers, we most likely often feel depressed and do not have a strong drive or love for life. In other words, we were not properly grounded.

One symptom of an unbalanced root chakra is food obsessions, eating disorders and other kinds of addictions. This is not to blame our parents or caregivers. This is actually the light we need to see; why we feel the way we feel and learn how to fix it, by taking full responsibility and getting off the wheel of blame and pain.

By now you should already be very familiar with your inner child. You now know that if she is not ok, nobody around you is. I suggest not hurrying up to the next chapters if you are not effortlessly communicating back and forth with your inner child in a very loving, respectful and kind way.

Although it is always a process and we can find things to change later, your inner child needs to feel totally like she fits in with you. It should feel like we are really turning things around for us. Peace should effortlessly begin to show up.

Before we move to the next chapters and working on

SETTING MYSELF FREE FROM MY OWN MIND.

healing the next stage of our lives, we are going to do a meditation for a couple of days. My suggestion is at least seven days in a row.

ACTIVITY 12

If you have come this far and you already know your inner child, there are big chances you already know at a conscious level what it was that hurt her so much. It could be a dramatic event or as simple as, she just did not feel loved or approved. If you are still not sure, before you do this meditation, go back to meet her and ask, "When was the very first time you assumed or concluded you were not good enough?" Pay close attention. This is when a lot of false information was recorded in her subconscious mind and from where you are living now.

I believe that any trauma, as stupid as it sounds, had an effect on us. If we still remember the trauma it is because we have not dealt with it and it is still affecting us. Unfortunately, growing up, we believed so many lies as if they were literal. Example: a mother that repeatedly says to her daughter, "If you do not obey, I will sell you at the market." The mom had no clue the child had no capacity to know this was a tactic to scare her, however never meant literally. The problem is that the child believed it and no wonder, as an adult, has panic attacks every time she gets close to a market. Before we do this Utopia (ages 0-7) meditation we need to have a very clear idea of what happened to us from age 0 to 7 that landed us where we are now. Most likely our depression now has a lot more to do with a trauma experienced when we were young than an experienced event that happened as an adult, but everyone is different.

We are going to stand up this time, which will help us to not fall asleep. We are going to spread our feet a little

SETTING MYSELF FREE FROM MY OWN MIND.

bit to maintain balance because I am going to ask you to close your eyes. So close your eyes and begin deep breathing. With each breath we are going to see light in and darkness out. At this moment we do not need to know what it is that we are exhaling.

Just know that any low vibe energy that does not help you to be happy and healthy will now leave. If you have experience, your intuition will tell you where the energy is leaving from and what it is. Example: I saw a huge dark spot in my stomach area leaving and when I asked what it was, the word "control" came to my mind. I also saw some low vibe energy leaving my knees, representing resentment. Just trust the process and feel like you are inhaling life and exhaling death.

Breathe in light, exhale darkness. Breathe in high vibe and exhale low vibe. As you are doing this I want you to see this light entering from your head and going all the way to the bottom of your spine and turning around up creating a big oval. As you do these, with your eyes closed, roll your eyes backwards. (This is a hypnosis tool.) Do these as long as you need and let it all go.

Begin focusing on your face, relax your forehead and then relax your jaw. Move to your neck and shoulders and consciously relax them. Repeat all this until you end up relaxing your toes. Take your time and do not continue until you believe you are as relaxed as you are going to get.

Once you are there, begin focusing on the bottom of your spine and see the color "red". I want you to visualize (imagine) yourself the very day you were born, immersed in a red environment. We already know what kind of life we experienced and what this life; we lived on our childhood produced as adults. In order to change our life now, we are going to have to reprogram our subconscious mind. So we are going to change our childhood into a childhood of perfection or 'utopia-childhood', using our imagination.

Our subconscious mind does not know if what we are

SETTING MYSELF FREE FROM MY OWN MIND.

imagining did happen or not, just as when we dream, we feel as it is happening. Our subconscious mind will see our imagination as something that is happening and will produce the right feelings that go with it; therefore producing the right connections in our brain.

We are going to imagine our perfect/utopia life from ages 0-7. We are going to imagine perfect supportive and encouraging parents, family members and siblings. If you have a hard time imagining your parents (or one parent) being good to you, it is ok; imagine yourself as an adult re-parenting your own baby/child. It is your story; there is no right or wrong ways of doing this.

We are going to imagine our first days at school as if everything went perfectly well. We are going to imagine that all of our physical and emotional needs were perfectly met at all times. If you happened to have had experienced any trauma at that age, go ahead and fix it. Talk to your inner child and fix it. Bring truth to the situation. Or just plain imagine that the trauma did not happen at all and your "adult you" protected you and the trauma did not even happen.

It might feel like we are lying, but we are not. This is the truth of how things should have been and are if all of humanity was emotionally healthy. This new way of seeing or imagining things will re-record our subconscious mind with new healthy patterns in our brain that will effortlessly produce a life of peace and joy in our now.

Finish your meditation when ready and come back to it as many times as needed, as you feel totally comfortable and the new story coming easily to your mind, like it really happened.

End your meditation with the light in your spine and open your eyes when you are ready. Do this meditation three times a day for at least seven days. This will eventually be step one of a seven step meditation. So get ready and enjoy.

13 OUR RELATIONSHIPS MIRROR OUR SELF-ESTEEM
GETTING OUR POWER BACK!

We are going to begin healing our young teen. This age group can be 8-13 or 14. We are talking about end of elementary and middle school years. Just remember to honor your feelings and go as slow or as fast as you think is best for you.

Most likely, if your physical and emotional needs were not met in your childhood, there are big chances that your puberty years didn't go good as well. Everyone is different; I would bet that things did not get magically healed at this age span if no one showed us the way of self-loving/healing. I am going to ask of you to not be so hard on yourself and not to judge yourself. Remember, we did the best we could and we should be very proud we survived.

Chances are that if we did not feel loved and approved in our childhood, at this age, we began to find a way to get approved. This is when the codependency patterns began in our brain. We began focusing on who we **thought** we needed to be, and we forgot to be ourselves. We began the painful path of self-consciousness and disconnected with our heart and feelings.

In this chapter we are going to take a look at our relationships with others. This is not the chapter where we focus on having better relationships. This is a chapter in which we will focus on our relationships with others to gather information about ourselves. This is the window to our soul.

When you relate to others, are you mostly trying to

change them, control them, so you feel better about yourself? Are you the one always feeling that no one does anything right but you? Do you unconsciously think that everyone should be doing this and that to fill your emotional and physical needs? You get the picture. Are you controlling yourself in your relationships? How comfortable do you feel in your relationships? Do you feel comfortable in your own skin and allow yourself to express freely? Or are you so self-conscious that you micro-manage everything you say and do? Are your relationships free or stressful?

Most likely, if our emotional needs were not met before, we made patterns in our brain to try and be what we **thought** we needed to be and do, in order to get someone else's approval. So these brain patterns continued getting stronger with time. I believe it was at this age that we stopped allowing ourselves to feel. We began oppressing our feelings because they were telling us the truth. Our feelings were loud and clear that we were letting others abuse us, but we chose not to pay attention so we could continue to please whoever we **thought** needed to love and like us.

Why did we decide to ignore our feelings? I happen to believe that it was because no one modelled to us that our feelings were actually our inner guidance. We were young, we had no clue of what was happening, we did the best we could to survive, and we created coping mechanisms to somehow feel a little better in our situation. Little did we know that this was going to backfire later in life.

Just to be clear, how did all this begin? I think it began by our main caregivers controlling us. Somehow they felt that we needed to be and do what they **thought** we needed to be and do, with good intentions they said, and began to control and manipulate us. But we somehow internalized that control and began controlling ourselves. Most likely with the same perceptions (ideas of who we needed to be and do) that was passed on to us by our

SETTING MYSELF FREE FROM MY OWN MIND.

caregivers. In my case my mom thought and communicated to me that it was important for me to be thin. I internalized that same control and I began controlling what I ate at this age.

The perception that being thin -in order to be happy- was passed to me by my mother and then as expected, I developed an eating disorder at this age span. I have mentioned before, if you now feel abandoned it is not your parents that are abandoning you now (the past does not exist anymore except in our minds). It is now you abandoning you. Same with control, if we were controlled in our childhood, it is now us controlling us and making us feel miserable. The good news is we can change ourselves, our perceptions and our thinking.

In a previous chapter we worked on allowing ourselves to feel again and to honor our feelings. In this chapter we are going to take a look at our relationships in order to find out if we are still losing ourselves or not. Are we still codependent? What is codependency? Codependency is to depend on others or circumstances outside of ourselves to feel good about ourselves.

This is the chapter we are going to take a look at our relationships and end those that do not serve us well. Do not be scared if, for the moment, you have to remove yourself from some of your relationships. You are changing and many will not like the new you. Those who are used to stepping all over you, will not like the new you. We are going to work on removing all masks and present ourselves as we are and honor what we feel in front of others. We are not going to hide our feelings and struggles anymore. Keeping secrets that produce shame has never worked for anyone. If you pretend to be happy all the time, but in reality you suffer with depression. This is the time that you will begin sharing the true you with struggles and all. It is time to be real. This is the kind of love that heals, when you are allowing yourself to be you, and some stay and love you.

SETTING MYSELF FREE FROM MY OWN MIND.

This is the time we are going to work on getting our power back and decide who we want to relate with. We are not going to focus on being what we **think** we need to be, in order to fit in. We are going to focus on being ourselves and we will find out with whom we really fit in, when we no longer lose ourselves. We matter.

ACTIVITY 13

This activity will require for you to be honest. I want you to get a piece of paper and write all the names with whom you have meaningful relationships. Next to their name you will write 0 to 10, how much you allow yourself to be you with that person and totally feel at peace in that relationship. I think that what you will discover this week will be very eye opening.

After you are done here, you are going to meditate and ask your young teen what is preventing her from being herself? What is keeping her from freely expressing herself? What are her fears? Does she fear that others won't like her if she is herself and show others her real self? If this is the case, which was mine, you are going to have to begin encouraging her to be herself without any type of control and then to see what happens. Tell her to pay attention and see who leaves and who stays. You are going to have to help that young teen inside of you to confront her fears. Ask her, "What happens if so and so doesn't like you? Are you going to die without them? What else happens?" Listen to what she answers and guide her into finally concluding that she is whole (with or without others) and nothing happens if another individual likes her or not.

It is easy for us, as adults, to know that if someone does not like us, nothing happens and we are totally ok. At that age the fear was real. We still have this fear at a

SETTING MYSELF FREE FROM MY OWN MIND.

subconscious level. So talk to her. Tell her you are giving her her own power back and it is up to her to decide who she wants and who she doesn't want in her life. It is not up to others to like her or not, tell her you like her and that is enough. Tell her we are whole and while we desire relationships, we really do not need them because we have each other (we have ourselves) and we are as whole as we are ever going to be. Encourage her to take baby steps and remove all masks, be true to herself and be honest with herself and others about her struggles. Encourage her to be herself and then to observe (not to control!) the outcome. Let us have fun seeing the true colors of so many around us. Let this activity be a fun one. I doubt it all can be done in seven days. This is a process. This is when we get our power back and decide who we want in our lives, not the other way around. Ask her what is so scary about unleashing all of herself? Confront the deepest fears. We are not victims; we always have power and options, only we didn't know it.

Another meditation I want you to do here, during this week, while you are already in the altered state of the mind, is to have a vision of your soul coming back to your body. Many of us, after years of not allowing ourselves to feel, got disassociated with our own physical body.

Doing this meditation will totally help and then, once we are inside our body; we are going to focus on -what does it feel to be ourselves and what is the worst case scenario if we allow ourselves to feel and be ourselves?

Confront your deepest fears. If you are still struggling with not controlling your feelings, try to do it a few hours at a time. See what happens? Did your worst case scenario happen? Probably not. Are you ok if you give yourself permission to feel?

I believe the reason we are so afraid to feel is because we down deep know, we are going to have to take full responsibility and change some things and probably end some toxic relationships. Confront the fear, what is the

SETTING MYSELF FREE FROM MY OWN MIND.

worst thing that can happen to you if you end this relationship? I totally know that change is scary and some relationships cannot end in one day or even a week, but guess what? If we are not happy, change is good!

"A lot of parents will do anything for their kids, except let them be themselves." Banksy

14 GETTING OUR PASSION BACK

This week we are going to take a peek at what it was that made us lose our passion. What is it that we liked doing in our childhood? What were our dreams? What caused us to not be who we wanted to become because we tried to be who others **thought** we needed to be? Where can we find our blue prints again? What is the one thing that we were created for and that could make us happy and give us effortless energy in our daily lives? When did we stop dreaming? Who said we couldn't do it? Who said we were not meant to be the best at what we love doing? Did we forget what we love doing? Who said to you that you will never make money being a _____?

Most of you reading this book are now adults who need to make a living; we all do. Some make good money, some do not. I think making a living is not the issue here. The issue is what kind of life we want to live. What do we want/like doing that gives us passion? What would we invest our life into that after twenty years we still love doing it? What is the goal here? To make money, or to find our passion and do what we love and make money doing it? I think, we all know the answer to this.

Do not feel afraid that you missed the train. It is never too late to begin doing and creating what we like and were created to do. What about going back to school and get certified in the area you always wanted to? Do we have options or are we powerless to change what we do? Yes, we might not be able to change in a day or even a year, but we do need to begin making small steps in the direction of our dreams.

I believe the trick here is to being allowing ourselves to dream, feel and create once again. Dream big, use your

SETTING MYSELF FREE FROM MY OWN MIND.

imagination.

ACTIVITY 14

We are going to ask ourselves: What made me lose my passion? Why am I not going after my passion? What is my passion to begin with? Do I have options? Can I begin taking online classes at night? Can I start creating, painting, or dancing? Who told me I couldn't do what I wanted to do? What was I really created to do? What makes me happy when I do it? What gives me a high? What would I do even if I didn't get paid for it? What comes natural to me?

After you are confronted with some truth and the blue prints of your being, make a decision to daily make small steps in the direction of your dreams. Allow yourself to dream big.

It is about time we explore creative self-expression and be who we were meant to be. Pick an activity you are interested in and maybe always wanted to do and give it a go. Think of what you want to express or create and do it. Can this eventually turn into your business? Yes it can. We have to start at some point.

SETTING MYSELF FREE FROM MY OWN MIND.

15 ACCEPTING OUR SEXUALITY

How many of us had a positive view of sex growing up? Let us be honest. Most of us who grew up under religion and now have to work with a lot of wrong perceptions about sex.

Why is talking about orgasms a taboo? If we are sexual human beings why is it such a taboo in many social groups to talk about pleasure, sex and orgasms? This week we are going to focus on our perceptions passed on to us about sex. Do they include shame and guilt? Were we encouraged to have pleasure or did we feel guilty for feeling pleasure?

No other subject arises more controversy as the subject of sexuality. Why is the subject of sexuality such a taboo? Have you ever thought of that? Why doesn't anyone talk freely about sexuality and orgasms? Why is there so much shame and guilt attached to sexuality? Who is at fault here, our culture, religion (indoctrination), society?

Our sexuality began developing around our eight's birthday and probably became active at the age of puberty. Our imagination developed and our body got ready for procreation. It might be little different for everyone, but I have a surprise for you, every human being is a sexual being. Whether we were positively instructed or not instructed at all in this area, we all became aware of our sexuality one way or another. Unfortunately for many, feelings of guilt and shame were often associated with sexuality creating trauma. "If pleasure is wrong, but I desire pleasure, there must be something wrong with me.", many of us concluded. And for some others who experienced sexual physical and emotional abuse even

SETTING MYSELF FREE FROM MY OWN MIND.

more unfortunate.

I am not here to say what is right and wrong for you. I am here to tell you that you need to find out what is right for you and to make up your mind and conclusions about your sexuality. All I know is that your sexuality is here to stay and it is way better to experience pleasure than pain, guilt and shame. I am here to say that sex is not only normal it is good and a great source of healing, both physical and emotional.

I do not know if you are heterosexual, bisexual, gay or lesbian. I do not know if you are transsexual, what I do know is that society and religion indoctrinated many of us and associated guilt and shame with our sexuality; and even more if you were not heterosexual. I am here to tell you that there is nothing wrong with any of us and our sexuality. And if we ever want to experience effortless pleasure, peace and joy within, it is going to have to start with accepting our own sexuality, in spite of what culture or religions say.

I grew up catholic and somehow the belief was that it is wrong to be anything other than heterosexual. It was not until my own daughter shared with me that she was gay that I began to look into this. I still carried all the shame and guilt religion put in my mind. I began to search by watching a movie, "Prayers for Bobby" which was a huge eye-opener for me. I then went ahead and watched a documentary called, "For the Bible tells me so". I can't be grateful enough for those who produced both of these shows. I ended up writing a book which is called, "Gays are not going to hell - the shocking truth about 'homosexuality' and the bible."

I wanted to write about this in hopes of helping any mother out there that is concerned with their gay ending in hell. Very few know that "homosexuality" is briefly mentioned only six times in the entire bible. The fact of this reality should at least be an indication of the lack of importance the writers of the bible gave to

SETTING MYSELF FREE FROM MY OWN MIND.

"homosexuality". If this was a definitive law about who enters heaven or hell for eternity wouldn't you think that all the writers would have written about it? Wouldn't have Jesus, of all people, at least mentioned it? He didn't. The sad part is while the bible is almost quiet on the subject of "homosexuality", our churches are not. I did my own bible study that took me about a year or two and I wrote about every single time the bible mentions "homosexuality". I came to the conclusion that it was considered normal to be gay in those times. I also do not believe in heaven or hell as "being places". I do believe in heaven and hell now as states of our mind. (More on how I came to this conclusion, in my book, "Oneness".) I also know that many gays now live in hell because they have not accepted themselves and still feel there is something wrong with them. Do not judge me for believing this way. Do not judge gays, if you have not done your own search within. Just remember, the truth will always set us free, exalt all and never divide. I am all about love, equality and lack of judgement.

This was a tough chapter to write; because of the persecution that sex has under religion and society. All I am saying here is that it is about time we accept all, including ourselves. It is about time someone talks to women about orgasms and how to have them. The internet is filled with stories of women in their forties who have not experienced an electric orgasm beginning in the bottom of their spine and ending up in their heads and extremities through all their nervous system. Is it ok for a woman to live and die without orgasms? Why? Why not? What is keeping you from enjoying pleasure? Take an honest look at your belief system about your own sexuality and be honest about how it is affecting you now. Is this an area you need to spend a week on?

WHAT ABOUT SEXUAL ADDICTIONS?

Many people believe it was at this age that addictions

SETTING MYSELF FREE FROM MY OWN MIND.

began. I believe this to be true. This is when we really began acting on all those coping mechanisms and brain patterns we formed at an earlier age. This is going to be the time we look into our addictions too. Many are daily addicted to anything that brings temporary pleasure such as food, sex, work, drugs, gambling, shopping, etc. Self-destructive patterns will not change until we fix all our traumas including sexual traumas. Let us take an honest look at our addictions. Keeping secrets kills us inside. Maybe this is the time we come out of the closet and share with others and/or ask for professional help. Let us meditate. Are my addictions affecting me and my loved ones? What is this addiction providing for me? What is the deep root of my addiction, when did it start, what was I feeling when it started? Am I trying to numb myself so I do not feel? Are those feelings so overwhelming? What is it that I am afraid to feel? Why? How is this working for me?

Pleasures are not the root of addictions. Some enjoy shopping, some become addicted to shopping. Shopping, sex and wine are definitely not the issue. The root of addiction is that somehow some were not loved and approved as they were growing up and created a void within. The brain patterns to create dopamine for feeling good about themselves were not there. Addictions began as we were trying to feel good and fill the void within with pleasures that can only satisfy temporarily, but they usually end up creating consequences that hurt us and others around us.

The solution to all is to find pleasure within. Buddha said something like this before he died: "Do not worship me, and find the light inside of yourself". Jesus said: "The kingdom of God (heaven) is inside." Many of our voids will get filled and as a result many circumstances in our life will improve on their own, as we begin this path of self-love and begin to honor all of ourselves and our feelings. Some of us would need professional help. It is totally ok to ask for help. Do not add shame or guilt to mental disorders. Do not be so hard on yourself and be very proud you have survived and are asking for help now.

ACTIVITY 15

Deep breathe and reach the altered state of the mind. Visualize your inner child in the puberty years and tell her it is totally ok and normal to be a sexual being. Tell that we all deserve pleasure in all manifestations: playing, creating, sex, etc. by using all of our five senses. Restricting our pleasure could have caused depression in our lives, so apologize to her and explain that you are learning now. Pleasure is not only normal; it is amazing and necessary for a healthy life. Meditate on what beliefs, ideas and prejudices towards your sexuality were passed on to you? How is that working in your life now? This might be a good time to speak about them with a good friend or a trusted counselor.

Homework: You have a full week to think where you want to go with your sexual life. Are you enjoying sex without guilt and shame? If not, why not? Who told you it was wrong? Is it wrong? How do you want to experience sex from now on? Totally up to you.

SETTING MYSELF FREE FROM MY OWN MIND.

16 UTOPIA MEDITATION AGES 8-14 / PUBERTY

SACRAL CHAKRA – UNBALANCED WHEN HAVING SEXUAL STRUGGLES OR DIFFICULTY FEELING JOY, OR EVEN FEELING AT ALL.

Often the sacral chakra becomes unbalanced after suffering from feelings of unworthiness and an unbalanced root chakra by age seven. Negative emotions are sometimes so strong that we built a wall to protect our feelings and avoid overwhelming emotional pain. This is sometimes referred to as a heart wall. People who have a large heart wall seem emotionally unavailable.

Unfortunately when we avoid our emotions our soul becomes disconnected from our bodies, causing a fragmented body and life, effortlessly producing anxiety and depression. It was then that we either went after the pleasure to fill our inner needs (later becoming an addiction) or we decided to block pleasure due to extreme feelings of guilt and shame. Some may become cold and unable to enjoy sex, others may become promiscuous. Either way, this chakra is usually blocked as a result of a blocked root chakra.

By now, you should already be very familiar with your inner young teen. You now know that if she is not ok nobody around you is, including you.

I suggest not hurrying up to the next chapters if you are still not on the side of your inner child. If you still have power issues and want to control her because you think you know better, stay with her and take your time.

SETTING MYSELF FREE FROM MY OWN MIND.

We have a life ahead of us. All these traumas were not created in a day. Do your meditations and go from there. It does not have to be perfect to move on. It just needs to feel like we are definitely turning things around and you are beginning to experience effortless joy and peace. Baby steps into a lifetime of change is way better than no change at all.

Before we move to the next chapters and the next stage of our lives, we are going to do a meditation for a couple of days. My suggestion is at least seven days in a row.

ACTIVITY 16

Same as activity 12, we are going to focus, create and imagine with the help of our right hemisphere our perfect utopia life from ages 8-14. We are going to see ourselves enveloped in orange at all times.

INSTRUCTIONS FOR ALL UTOPIA MEDITATIONS. (Skip if you already know what you are doing.)

We are going to stand up this time, which will help us to not fall asleep. We are going to spread our feet a little bit to maintain balance because I am going to ask you to close your eyes. So close your eyes and begin deep breathing. With each breath we are going to see light in and darkness out. At this moment we do not need to know what it is that we are exhaling. Just know that any low vibe energy that does not help you to be happy and healthy will now leave. Just trust the process and feel like you are inhaling life and exhaling death. Breathe in light, exhale darkness. Breathe in high vibe and exhale low vibe. As you are doing this I want you to see this light entering from your head and going all the way to the bottom of your spine and turning around up creating a big oval. As you do these, with your eyes closed, roll your eyes backwards. (This is a hypnosis tool.) Do these as long as you need and let it all go.

Begin focusing on your face, relax your forehead and then relax

SETTING MYSELF FREE FROM MY OWN MIND.

your jaw. Move to your neck and shoulders and consciously relax them. Repeat all this until you end up relaxing your toes. Take your time and do not continue until you believe you are as relaxed as you are going to get.

Once you are there, begin focusing on the next area up from your spine, your entire pelvis area and see the color "orange". I want you to visualize (imagine) yourself at the ages around 8-14. Do not force the vision, let it come freely. Depending on the age she is presenting herself, is where you are now at the maturing emotional process.

We are going to see ourselves at that certain age allowing ourselves to feel. We are going to include ourselves (as adults) in our vision. We are going to model the self-re-parenting method and our subconscious will make new and healthier brain-patterns and connections. We are going to see our adult telling our teen that it is totally ok to feel and to trust her feelings. You are going to support and encourage her to keep believing and trusting herself. Many of us were made to feel that our feelings were incorrect. But feelings are always right on target. If she felt abused and abandoned, she was. Tell her that.

See as how she honored and respected herself, those around her did the same. See her not allowing any disrespect from others. Be there in the vision and always be her biggest fan and encourager. See her making decisions and choices about who she wants to relate with and be around. See her going after her passion. Her feelings matter, her dreams and passions matter. See her dancing, painting or learning about her passion. See her dreaming of the life ahead as a doctor, lawyer, artist, etc. (whatever she wanted to be). Tell her we can still make it happen. It is never too late to go after our dreams. We matter.

See her having pleasure and not feeling guilt or shame. Tell her every human being is a sexual being and it is normal. Encourage her to accept her sexuality and to

SETTING MYSELF FREE FROM MY OWN MIND.

forgive all well intentioned people that associated guilt and shame with it. Tell her it is ok and you are here for her to help her relearn a healthy approach about her sexuality. Mean it. Tell her it is ok to accept the changes in her body and to accept it as a gift. Tell her you are with her to help her embrace pleasure. Tell her anything else that comes to your mind.

By now you should have enough experience to change and make your own meditations that suit you the best way. My ideas might not be the perfect ones for you. We are all different. Do what is best for you.

It might feel like we are lying, but we are not. This is the truth of how things should have been if our main care givers were emotionally healthy. This new way of seeing or imagining things will re-record our subconscious mind with new healthy patters in our brain that will effortlessly produce a life of peace and joy in our now.

Finish your meditation when you are ready but come back to it as many times as needed until you feel totally comfortable and the new story coming easily to your mind, like it really happened. End your meditation with the light in your spine and open your eyes when you are ready. Do this meditation three times a day for at least seven days.

You can also begin to make affirmations like: "I allow myself to feel. I have healthy boundaries. I do not allow others to walk all over me. I have power and options at all times. I am not a victim. I can decide who I want to be friends with and who I want to be around on my daily living. I honor and embrace my inner passion. I allow myself to freely express myself and be creative. I value and respect my body. My sexuality is sacred." Whatever works for you, is perfect!

The result of this aligned sacral chakra is:
- Passionate
- Present in their body
- Sensual

SETTING MYSELF FREE FROM MY OWN MIND.

- Creative
- Connected to their feelings
- Emotionally stable
- Feeling joyful most of the time.

SETTING MYSELF FREE FROM MY OWN MIND.

17 LETTING GO OF UNHEATHY RELATIONSHIPS AND OLD BELIEF SYSTEMS

WE CANNOT GET HEALED IN THE SAME ENVIRONMENT THAT WE GOT SICK.

We are going to go through the toughest part of our recovery. Up to now it was about finding out the lies that have been driving our lives and the truth that sets us free.

The following chapters are about doing and putting in to action what we have been learning so far and taking full responsibility for our lives. The victim mentality has to end and we need to stop blaming others and circumstances about our life. So get ready and take your time. Baby steps are more than perfect.

By now you know that who we think we are and what we effortlessly manifest and experience now is usually the consequence of our earlier years. I am not here to point fingers or blame others, I am here to tell you that we need to take full responsibility and act accordingly. I am also here to tell you that we all should be very proud of ourselves for surviving (up to now!) and are now taking the path of self-love and self-respect that eventually will lead us to full recovery.

If we, as a child, experienced strict upbringing, controlling and authoritarian parents, bullying, physical or emotional abuse and/or were indoctrinated with disempowering theology, we either became totally passive and allowed the world to take us wherever, or we became totally aggressive and controlling. We felt helpless either way and thought we were victims. We did not know we had the power to change things back then, but it is now time we empower ourselves and change our lives.

The first thing we are about to do in this chapter is to remove ourselves from any relationship that is not helping. I want you not to worry about being lonely. It is our time to heal and it is ok to spend time alone. Either way, who needs relationships where we are being used and/or oppressed? I want to reassure that, after you are done with this self-love process, you are going to attract very many healthier relationships. I happen to believe that we attract at the same level of our self-esteem. If you have issues, you are attracting others with issues. So as we get healed we are going to begin attracting and be attracted to healthier individuals and our relationships will effortlessly work.

We are going to remove ourselves from the environment that made us sick in the first place. If, when you visit your parents, you feel like a 7-8 year old and in the same powerless situation, how about you stop visiting and love them from a distance? I am not saying this is a permanent situation but you definitely are going to lose and leave many behind. As you begin acting on your new self-love attitude it is you who will not want to be around many. Follow the lead of your heart. If you go to the usual monthly get together and observe and you begin feeling, "what am I doing here?", follow the lead of your heart and leave. No guilt! Your self-healing process comes first at this moment.

Remove yourself from all critical and negative people. If you can't cut ties permanently, try your best to keep a distance from them at least for the moment. Find some supportive people. Begin to be honest about your struggles and others will begin sharing too. Invite them to do this process with you and help each other. When you take the courage to be you, struggles and all, observe who stays. Those are your true friends, stay close to those. Their unconditional love for you will heal you from the inside out. Remember, you decide who stays and who goes away in your life. You choose! You have options and power. It

SETTING MYSELF FREE FROM MY OWN MIND.

is your life, own it.

After spending some time thinking about who needs to go and acting accordingly, we are going to take a look at our attachments. What are attachments? Everyone or anything we **think** we **need** to be happy or survive. We are going to end our codependency to circumstances, feelings, people and old belief systems. Buddha said, "The root of all fear is attachment". I want you to know that you are whole with or without others, money, perfect circumstances, a perfect job, a perfect family, and certain beliefs. Set yourself free and begin questioning it all.

Not everything that was taught to us was true. The way to know if our belief system is truth is just to take a look at our lives. How is it working? Are you still struggling with the belief system that there is nothing good in you? How is that working? Are you willing to let go and find out truth that serves you and sets you free? Didn't Jesus say: "By their fruit you will recognize them"? What is the fruit he was talking about, the fruit of the spirit? Joy, peace, love, etc. If you are not effortlessly experiencing the above fruit, what if what we believe is not necessarily the truth?

In my book called, "Oneness", I shared my path out of bondage from a theology of separation (duality). You do not have to walk my path; just take a look at your own belief system. If it is working then do nothing, but if you are experiencing anxiety and depression, your belief system is not working. Do something about it. The internet is a great tool to search. Just be careful and follow your inner peace. Open your mind and listen to the younger generation without judgment. Only listen to those that are experiencing the fruit. Do not listen to anyone that is not effortlessly manifesting peace, love, joy, health, etc.

ACTIVITY 17

SETTING MYSELF FREE FROM MY OWN MIND.

I am going to ask you to do lots of meditating and to decide who needs to stay and who needs to go, at least momentarily. Deal with fears of being lonely. Know the ones that have been using you will not like the new you and that is totally ok. Keep choosing you. You do not have to explain to everyone what you are doing. The ones that really care for you will be happy you are finally taking care of yourself. If one or two friends stay, that is great. Let all others go. Stop watering plants that do not water you. Stop being the first one to text and see if they notice it and looked for you. Stop trying to please others and begin pleasing you. Stop wanting to solve other's problems and be used by others. Spend all your energy discovering what pleases you and do it.

In those relationships that you chose to keep, learn to set healthy boundaries. Learn to respect yourself and stand your ground. Be honest and learn to say "no thank you." in a respectful way. Be honest, tell them you do not like the way they ____ to you. See if they stay or leave the new you.

I want you to be aware that when you start questioning your belief system (mostly indoctrination from religion, traditions and society) persecution will show up. People will say all sorts of things about you. Face the fear of criticism and rejection from others. If you love yourself you will actually allow yourself to get angry if they disrespect you, it will be lots easier to leave the relationship. It is very hard to leave many behind that have been friends for a long time. There is definitely a price to pay for our own wellbeing and freedom. It is your choice. I chose me.

I didn't go with just any new belief system out there. I opened my mind and heart and began finding answers within. I followed the path of peace. If it did not bring peace, that was not it. The truth radically loves and does not divide. The truth sets us free. Any belief system that points at finding the solution outside of ourselves is just

SETTING MYSELF FREE FROM MY OWN MIND.

another religion using different "lingo".

Everything that points at a wonderful future but not a wonderful present with who you are and have is also another religion using new "lingo". Trust your heart at all times. The path to your own heart is a scary one but with amazing fruit. Like I said before, only listen to those that are experiencing effortlessly joy and peace, pay attention to their fruit. No fruit, do not listen. Keep searching.

I want to tell you that I am beyond proud of you if you made it this far. A life of autonomy and wholeness is worth living.

As we come to discover that we are whole no matter what, we begin effortlessly loving others. We don't have the need to control or manipulate people or circumstances. We **want** to be surrounded by good people, we do not **need** them; big difference. As we believe this, our actions will follow. We do not ever beg for love. We are whole and we enjoy all those that love us and want to be close to us. We let go of all others. Is this painful? You bet. There will be some grieving to be done here. Choose you!

Never, ever beg for love. Never beg someone to be with you. Never beg for attention, commitment, affection, time and effort. Never beg for someone to come back or stay. You should never have to ask to feel wanted. Begging is demanding and degrading. If someone doesn't willingly give you these things, whit their arms wide open, they are not for you. No one, under any circumstances is ever worth begging for.
Anonymous

You are whole and worthy of love!

SETTING MYSELF FREE FROM MY OWN MIND.

SETTING MYSELF FREE FROM MY OWN MIND.

18 MAKING OUR DREAMS COME TRUE

This is the chapter where we bring back the knowledge of all our desires, passions and dreams discovered in previous chapters. This is the chapter where we will overcome the fear of failing and to begin moving forward in the direction of our dreams and desires. Many believe in the "Law of Attraction". I do believe in it, I just think many misunderstand what it means. Here is my take.

THE LAW OF ATTRACTION

This is what I believe. The Law of Attraction works 100% of the time. You want something. You figure out about your belief system in relationship to what you want. Because what we deeply believe and was recorded in our subconscious mind is manifested 100% of the time.

If our belief system does not match what we want at a vibrational level, it will never be manifested. Example: if you **deep down** believe that you are not worthy to receive it, it will never happen.

What we need to do is, change our belief system to match what we want, same vibration. Then we work very hard at it, without ever giving up. We fail and we begin again. We ask for help, we find new options and work at it again, while seeing yourself succeed during your meditations. You search for wisdom within. You ask within what you are still doing wrong and change, and work. Then, we get it, it finally happens and it manifests. And usually, by the time we get it we did not **need** it anymore. That is how I believe it happens 100% of the time.

SETTING MYSELF FREE FROM MY OWN MIND.

ACTIVITY 18

What are your dreams? Are they clear to you? Write them down. Make a list of things you would like to accomplish. They do not have to be related to a job or business. They can be as small as eating better, walking a mile a day, etc. It is your life, you choose.

You now are in charge of things you want to change and accomplish. Do not feel guilty for not having huge dreams. Then, see yourself being successful during your meditations this week. Begin to set some weekly or even daily goals. Baby steps. Afraid to fail? We all are. Overcome any fear and take appropriate actions in the direction of your goals. Take some risks and see what happens, small steps. If all you can do today is a search on line for new schools, that's good. If all you can do today is making a phone call to someone that might know about what you are searching for, it is ok. Do not be hard on yourself. Growing up is tough. A daily baby step in the direction of our dreams is good enough.

Write down your biggest dream on a piece of paper and make some goals. Now meditate and figure out if you deeply believe it can happen to you. Why not? Are you any different than many that have archived their goals? Why are you not good enough to make it happen or to even receive the blessing? Find out your belief system in relationship with this dream and yourself. Find some facts. Let go of all lies of unworthiness or that you are not smart, strong, pretty, etc., enough. Write down some truth that matches in a vibrational level with your dream. Example: "I am powerful enough to make things happen. I am good enough to receive every blessing this life has to offer." Read it every night before you go to bed and then see yourself being successful and making it happen. Feel the joy.

SETTING MYSELF FREE FROM MY OWN MIND.

During your meditation times, search for wisdom within; all answers are within. See yourself removing all obstacles. Then follow with action. Keep a notebook with your goals written in it and begin marking with a checkmark those fulfilled. Keep dreaming. Make it happen. You are not powerless!

SETTING MYSELF FREE FROM MY OWN MIND.

SETTING MYSELF FREE FROM MY OWN MIND.

19 WHAT ABOUT ANGER?

Some of us were so oppressed that we did not allow ourselves to feel/get angry. We were taught that being angry -and showing it- might not be very kind and/or lady-like. With this said there are two sides of the same coin. Many continue to oppress all feelings, including anger and continue to allow others walking all over them. The other side of the coin is the many that control and manipulate others using anger. Either way anger is just a feeling that has to be felt and properly dealt with. Anger is not the enemy, anger is the messenger. Most likely the feeling of anger is the product of someone abusing us. Anger needs to be dealt with as any other feeling.

I taught "Anger Management" classes for adults for a few years and the basic information I have for you is that we have to pay attention to our anger and not ignore it or keep it in. For all of us that did not allow ourselves to feel, the anger kept inside eventually came out in other self-destructive ways, such as anxiety or panic attacks. Either way, anger has to be dealt with and worked on at the moment it is happening. What I mean with this, is to pay attention to our anger and not to avoid it. Then, go ahead and ask ourselves why we are angry and uncover some truth. Most of the time, we are either angry at ourselves or others, or both. Most of the time, the anger is present because others are disrespecting us and we are allowing it. So this kind of information will help us make better choices and decisions and help us act accordingly.

A practice that has saved me very many headaches is to ask the other person when I feel anger, "And what exactly did you mean by what you just said or did?". We give the other person a chance to clarify and then we decide if we continue or discontinue this relationship. Many of the times the other person realizes he or she made a mistake and apologizes right there. Most of the time, it was a total misunderstanding and the other person has a chance to explain what he or she meant.

"I take zero percent disrespect", that is my new motto I live by. Allowing disrespect does not work for either me or anyone around me. It never ends right. My experience is that by oppressing my own anger and continuing in disrespectful relationships I usually end up with anxiety. That is not worthy for me. I continue to choose me.

Anger has a very bad reputation, but in reality it is just a messenger, so allow yourself to feel and explore as you become angry. If you, on the other hand, have a problem with using anger to control or manipulate others, you probably need to go back to work on your own voids and find out why you need to manipulate so that others meet your needs. Ask yourself: "Is it working?" The problem here might be an addiction accompanied with anger issues. Either way, this might be the time we do something about it and ask for professional help. What needs to be solved this week is to allow ourselves to get angry and act accordingly in a respectful and assertive way to fix our lives. Anger is not necessarily a bad thing. If we happen to see an adult abusing a child we will feel anger in us that will make us act accordingly and save the child. Anger is a healthy emotion; it just needs to be dealt with at the moment. Anger is the messenger, remember that.

ACTIVITY 19

Spend a week meditating on your anger. Do you allow yourself to feel angry? Do you brainwash yourself and convince yourself not to feel anger and do not change things in fear that we might lose some relationships?

SETTING MYSELF FREE FROM MY OWN MIND.

What would happen if you allow yourself to feel angry? Most likely you are going to have to set boundaries and change a few things. Do not be afraid of change, change is good.

Write down what has kept you angry for decades. What is so wrong in your life that makes you angry? Remember, you have options. Are there any relationships you need to end or set a new set of boundaries? What makes you angry on a daily basis? How are you handling the anger?

Are you keeping it in or are you letting it out to control and manipulate others? What can you do to change the way you view anger? What can you do to change the way anger affects you and your health? Is the feeling of anger telling you something? What?

Like I said, these are the chapters in which we are not only meditating; we are doing something about it. Why do we keep allowing others to disrespect us? Honor all of your feelings, including anger. Anger has a bad reputation but is here to help. If you have an abusive boss that keeps making you angry, what are your options? Can you start looking for another job?

Remember, in these chapters we are working very hard on breaking the victim mentality and taking full responsibility in our lives. We have power and always have options, only we forget most of the time. Stop seeing yourself as a victim.

You don't have to be positive all the time. It's perfectly okay to feel sad, angry, annoyed, frustrated, scared, or anxious.
Having feelings doesn't make you a "negative person". It makes you human.
Lori Deschene

SETTING MYSELF FREE FROM MY OWN MIND.

20 UTOPIA MEDITATION
AGES 14-21

SOLAR PLEXUS CHAKRA – UNBALANCED: STRUGGLING WITH THE "GUT FEELING" OF NOT FEELING GOOD EOUGH.

The solar plexus is a very powerful chakra because it is considered to be the seat of our emotions. This chakra is associated with our gut feeling of either knowing we are ok and worthy, or not feeling good enough and feeling unworthy. This drives our emotions and most of our actions, and this is why it is such a powerful chakra.

With a balanced solar plexus chakra we understand and know the truth about ourselves. Our actions will effortlessly produce a life of victory, as we believe we are worthy of all blessings this life (Universe/Love/ God) has to offer. On the contrary, when we believe so many lies about ourselves, this chakra will effortlessly produce actions that mirror our belief system (in this case that we do not deserve the good this life has to offer), producing our own hell on earth.

The result of unbalanced root and sacral chakras is, of course, an unbalanced solar plexus chakra. It was during this chakra's development, between the ages of 14-21, that we began to live with a "poor me" or "victim" mentality as a result of not taking responsibility in our life and blaming everything around us. We blamed people and we blamed circumstances, creating a life of pain and bondage because we felt powerless to change anything about it. It was also around this age when we learned that we had to be a "martyr", or put everyone else and their needs before ours in order to feel better about ourselves. This is where we began to put ourselves last and allow others to walk all over us. It is also here that many learned how to put others down as a temporary fix to make them feel better about themselves (bullies).

An unbalanced solar plexus is mirrored by a life of very low self-esteem, allowing others to walk all over us and/or control and manipulation to others to fill our needs. There is no need for me to tell you why it is so important to balance this chakra. Life will begin to get significantly better and our relationships will also get significantly better once we take full responsibility and we begin making better choices. There is a whole life ahead of us once we quit waiting for the change to come from the outside of ourselves and begin to make changes happen.

By now we should have stopped blaming others and began to take full responsibility for our lives. We probably began making actual changes to our lives. This process will be a long one. We did not get where we are in a day and relationships and jobs can be very complicated to leave or change. But if we are in the process of making changes and taking better choices, we probably are ready to begin doing our utopia meditation for another 7 days and then move on to the following upper chakras. The best is yet to come, so do not be discouraged.

In these past few chapters we learned to move on with our power. We are not victims and always have options. You should have begun to feel lots better in your skin and effortlessly felt a lot less anxiety and depression. The goal of reprogramming our mind with this meditation that follows is to experience great confidence, autonomy and an inner drive that will continue to make your life better and better. We are not waiting for a god out there, the universe, others or circumstances to come and fix our lives; as adults we are fully responsible, working on fixing our lives ourselves, with the help and guidance of our inner wisdom.

SETTING MYSELF FREE FROM MY OWN MIND.

ACTIVITY 20

INSTRUCTIONS FOR ALL UTOPIA MEDITATIONS.
(Skip if you already know what you are doing.)
We are going to stand up this time, which will help us to not fall asleep. We are going to spread our feet a little bit to maintain balance because I am going to ask you to close your eyes. So close your eyes and begin deep breathing. With each breath we are going to see light in and darkness out. At this moment we do not need to know what it is that we are exhaling. Just know that any low vibe energy that does not help you to be happy and healthy will now leave. Just trust the process and feel like you are inhaling life and exhaling death. Breathe in light, exhale darkness. Breathe in high vibe and exhale low vibe. As you are doing this I want you to see this light entering from your head and going all the way to the bottom of your spine and turning around up creating a big oval. As you do these, with your eyes closed, roll your eyes backwards. (This is a hypnosis tool.) Do these as long as you need and let it all go.

Begin focusing on your face, relax your forehead and then relax your jaw. Move to your neck and shoulders and consciously relax them. Repeat all this until you end up relaxing your toes. Take your time and do not continue until you believe you are as relaxed as you are going to get.

Same as past utopia activities, we are going to focus and create and imagine with the help of our right hemisphere our perfect utopia life from ages 14-21. We are going to see ourselves enveloped in yellow at all times.

We are going to visualize ourselves at that certain age paying attention to our feelings and then taking a responsible action without fear. You will visualize yourself following your dreams and setting goals. You are going to see yourself doing it, whatever it is that you dream doing.
You are going to see yourself failing and feeling ok about your own failure. You are going to see yourself start again and working very hard until you achieve victory. You are

SETTING MYSELF FREE FROM MY OWN MIND.

going to not limit any of your dreams. You are going to be, in your vision, the most successful person that has ever walked on the planet making things happen and being very successful. Feel it. Feel the joy and feel very proud of yourself.

See yourself honoring all your feelings and only allowing healthy relationships. You see yourself setting healthy boundaries and you do not allow others to walk all over you and use you. You matter and you know that now. You will observe others that will criticize you but somehow it does not bother you one bit. You believe in yourself and you act accordingly. You know you are good at heart and you deserve every blessing this universe/god has to offer. You see yourself working hard. You see others working hard with you. You see the right relationships and the right connections coming to you and support you in your new endeavors. You will see yourself feeling totaling comfortable in your skin and full of confidence. You see yourself letting others free, not controlling or manipulating them. Only they know what is best for them. You stand up tall and feel so good about yourself even if not everyone approves of you or what you are doing. You follow your heart and no one else's.

You do not see yourself as a victim and you do not see yourself waiting for anyone or anything to come fix your life. You make your dreams come true, no one else. You begin to see yourself, not only full of power, but full of options, joy and peace.

Finish your meditation when you are ready and come back to it as many times as needed as you feel totally comfortable and the new story coming easily to your mind, like it really happened. End your meditation with the light in your spine and open your eyes when you are ready.

Do this meditation three times a day for at least seven days.

You can make these affirmations too, "I have the power to change things in my life. I have the power to

SETTING MYSELF FREE FROM MY OWN MIND.

change the things I do not like about my life. I have options and I am never powerless. All power and wisdom is within me. I love the person I am. I take full responsibility for my life. I am beginning to love my life. I stand up for myself and for what I believe. I never give up. It is ok to fail. It is ok to feel, my feelings are messengers. I act accordingly, focusing into what is best for me. I am courageous, I can and I will. I am changing things, my life matters". Whatever works for you, is perfect!

The result of this aligned solar plexus chakra is:
- We have the courage to change things
- Speak up for ourselves
- We have will power and self-control
- Autonomy
- Confidence
- Inner drive
- We feel in control without controlling others and circumstances
- The ability to master your thoughts
- Overcome fear
- Take appropriate action in any situation

Once you start seeing the results of self-improvement, it really becomes addicting. You start falling in love with the person you're becoming, the places you're going, the things you are doing, and it motivates you to work even harder.
Anonymous

SETTING MYSELF FREE FROM MY OWN MIND.

SETTING MYSELF FREE FROM MY OWN MIND.

21 DO WE REALLY, REALLY LOVE OURSELVES?

So far we have focused on our relationships to learn about ourselves. Then I asked you to quit all those toxic relationships that hurt you. I know that this is such a hard step in your recovery. We all carry so many preconceived ideas about how relationships should be, especially with our family members. If you had a bad relationship with your parents when you were growing up and they are still alive, chances are you still do not have a good relationship with them. But as we talked in the past chapter, we cannot get healed in the same environment that got us sick to begin with. And I am now recommending you to remove yourself from toxic family relationships, at least for the moment. We can learn to love from the distance.

On the chapters that follow we are going to work on our relationships, the ones you decided to keep. As you know by now, controlling and manipulating others to love us the way we need to be loved, did not work, and will never work. With this being said, we are going to focus big on our relationship with ourselves once again. Once we fix this at a heart level, our other (the new and the ones we decided to keep) relationships will all fall into place.

"***Love yourself first and everything else*** *falls into line. You really have to love yourself to get anything done in this world."*
Lucille Ball

Instead of focusing how compassionate we are with others, we are going to focus how compassionate we are with ourselves. In other words, if your struggle is having difficulty trusting others, I am going to ask of you to answer, "Do you trust yourself?" Remember, our outer world is the mirror of our inner world. So let us move on and fix our inner world to resemble heaven on earth.

The age we are going to be focusing on is 21-33. This is the last time we will focus on a certain age of our lives. From then on we will focus on spiritual matters, and as we all know, spirit has no age or even time limitations.

Many of us say we love ourselves but do we really, really love ourselves? Our actions, decisions and relationships model if we really do love ourselves or not. How many times we say we love ourselves but continue to put ourselves last in the list. How many times you find yourself doing things you -deep down- know you should not be doing? Remember, no one can truly give what they do not have and if it is not good for you, it is not good for anyone around you. So how to learn to love ourselves, I mean, truly love ourselves?

First we need to learn what unconditional love is. Unconditional love is the lack of judgment. Unconditional love is the love that heals our soul from our inside out. We stop judging all of ourselves and specially our feelings. We give ourselves permission to feel and honor all of our feelings and act accordingly without caring who likes us or not. It is when we are so one with our heart, so one with whom we are and we live from that state of complete peace. Many call this to be centered. How do you know if you are there? First of all you experience effortless peace at overwhelming levels and making decisions that benefit or bring pleasure come natural and easy, without any shame and/or guilt.

Emotions were not meant to be controlled or/and oppressed. Actually, that was the way we got disconnected with our self and the main root of anxiety, depression and disassociation. We need to give 100% freedom to ourselves to feel every single feeling. It seems we were taught to control a lot less, the entire positive (high vibrational) feelings such as happy ones. But for some, we

SETTING MYSELF FREE FROM MY OWN MIND.

were so negatively programmed at subconscious level that feeling happy might lead to feeling guilty and afraid. Always focusing and fearing for the other shoe to drop.

We were usually taught to -at all costs- avoid other (low vibrational) feelings such as sadness, fears, boredom, anger, jealousy, anxiety, depression, etc. Not knowing that this backfires and produces more of the same. We create what we focus on.

In order to go from a mind-led life to a spirit/heart led life we are going to have to get good at spending time alone in silence. We are so used to blocking our feelings that we do not know how to spend time alone. For now, I will ask you to confront all fears and spend a lot of time alone focusing on your feelings. Learn to love your company and listen within. Either way we look at it, the kingdom of heaven is within.

ACTIVITY 21

During this time, you are going to continue to meditate and meet your inner child. See what age she shows up this time. You might be working with your young adult now, but when in reference to feelings she might still show young. It is totally ok, tell her that you give her permission to feel. Ask her what she is feeling now. Do not oppress her answer. Go ahead and ask her why she feels this way?

As mentioned before, one of my tools that have kept me in peace for years now is to go meditate as soon as any situation makes me lose my peace. Sometimes I have no clue why I have an uneasy feeling. Is it something I said or plan to do? Is it something I am doing? Most of times it is clear to me why I am feeling fear, but not always. I meditate, listen within and then act accordingly and my peace comes back.

My peace is not for sale, and I go to great lengths to

keep it that way. I struggled with anxiety for decades and that is no longer an option for me.

Let me give you an example so this is clear. The minute I lose my peace, I meditate as soon as possible. Even a trip to the restroom will do so I can spend some time alone. I have got so good at this that with 1-3 deep breaths and little imagination, I am right there with my inner child. I ask, why do you feel this way? The answer comes as a thought. It could be, "You lost touch with your feelings and wantings because you are trying to please such and such." I go back to the situation with a different attitude and act accordingly, and peace overwhelms me again. Do not be so hard on yourself, remember, this is a process.

Embrace low vibe feelings. Just know that all those ugly feelings are here to stay and will get louder and even more uncomfortable until we learn the lesson. So we might as well listen and learn. Our feelings are and will never be our worst enemy. If you have anxiety and depression, chances are they will not go away until we get rid of the root of the problem within.

One of the emotions that is so healing is crying. For many, especially men, crying is not an option; they have been oppressing it for years. Just know that crying is normal and it is a process to heal our soul and if oppressed usually shows up as a bad temper or anger. You need to talk to your inner child if this is you, let her or him know that it is totally ok to cry. As practice, go ahead and watch a sad movie, watch how sometimes we are not even crying for what is happening in the movie, but for one or even more emotions we have kept inside of us. A good cry heals the soul. Allow yourself to cry as needed. Embrace your tears.

This may sound like an easy chapter. But I do believe this is a process for life. Being one with our true self will require a conscious process now that eventually, will turn to be an unconscious way of living that will effortlessly

SETTING MYSELF FREE FROM MY OWN MIND.

produce joy and peace. In other words, be totally 100% on your side at all times. Imagine what kind of life we would effortlessly have if we do this 24/7, if we really become our own best friend under every single circumstance.

Once you get good at really loving yourself it will show, you will get good at freely receiving love from others. Proud of you for embarking this life changing process of finding out, you are as important as everyone else is. You matter. You can focus on many other qualities of love, such as compassion, empathy, affection, giving, supporting, encouraging, forgiving, etc. but just know that all these effortlessly will show up after you truly begin to love yourself. When you truly love yourself, you stop judging yourself as good or bad (good an evil) and as you love yourself as you are, all these will effortlessly follow.

Can you love and not have compassion? And once you are compassionate towards yourself, as a result, you will effortless have compassion towards others. We can now give what we have.

In my book "Levels of awakening", I explained how the heart chakra or the love chakra was represented by Jesus (divine and human) in the bible. Our savior is and has always been: Divine/human love.

The reason I am bringing this up now is because nothing will ever get fixed without love. Love is the key we have been looking for decades. It is not the love from others to us, but the love to us from ourselves.

SETTING MYSELF FREE FROM MY OWN MIND.

SETTING MYSELF FREE FROM MY OWN MIND.

22 FORGIVING
LETTING GO OF ALL RESENTMENT

Forgiveness does not mean that you have to be friends again with the persons that hurt you. It does not even mean that you forgive what someone did to you. If it was wrong then, it is still wrong today.

The FORGIVENESS that sets you free is when you let go of the debt. You no longer spend your energy on trying to pay them back, change the other person or even teach them a lesson. You begin to trust the Universe (universal consciousness) to do its job perfectly, which is to mirror of their belief system.

The Universe will continue to present the lesson to be learned over and over, a lot better than what we could ever do. True forgiveness is when we allow the Universe to do its job, and we get out of the way, and we begin to use all our energy into learning our own lessons. For us, this was a lesson too.

When we understand this, we understand that there is no purpose for us to keep any low vibe energy (feelings) inside of us that is hurting us.

ACTIVITY 22

Write a list of people that you **think** have hurt you. If they come to mind it is because you are still holding that energy and/or resentment. Then know that this was exactly the mirror of your own self-esteem and forgive yourself. I totally understand that if you were hurt as a child, you were not responsible at all, so then go ahead and

SETTING MYSELF FREE FROM MY OWN MIND.

make peace within. Know that hurt people hurt others and set them free. Allow the Universe to do its job. Some will eventually search healing, some will choose to take medicines and die with depression and anxiety. It is up to them. Set them free.

Now (safely) burn the paper and watch it disappear. As you see the words disappear, visualize your resentment and forgiveness leaving your body.

23 DEALING WITH SHAME
IT IS NOT YOUR FAULT THAT YOU ARE STRUGGLING

Unfortunately shame is often linked or attached to mental issues and addictions. But I am here to tell you that it was not your fault. If anything, you should feel, is very proud of yourself for all coping mechanisms and how you have survived and are working on your recovery process.

The fact is that no one can successfully recover by shaming themselves and hiding their issues. Secrets kept within grew and kept us in bondage. The fact is that by hiding how we really are feeling is causing us to disconnect with our hearts even farther and makes matters worse and keeps us from asking for the help needed. It is not your fault that you developed those self-destructive patterns to survive trauma in your childhood. These mental illnesses are caused by a combination of factors that you were not responsible for and were not your choice. You are not weak and your worth has not been diminished. Children are not and will never be at fault. Most likely it was the parenting, indoctrination and society/culture we grew up in that were responsible for our pain, but we are not here to focus on the past. As we now know, we can't change our past, we are here to change our present.

The antidote to shame is to have the courage to be vulnerable. It is having the courage to take our masks off and say, "I am not ok at the moment". If we continue to be afraid of what others might think of us, it would make our issues grow and it is us who continue to suffer. So while it is very important to be real and share with others,

SETTING MYSELF FREE FROM MY OWN MIND.

in this chapter I will ask you to take a look at how much compassion and empathy you are having towards yourself.

First of all, we need to admit that it is really not fun to deal with anxiety, depression, fears, addictions and all sorts of mental disorders. No, it is not fun, but at some point we need to admit it was not our fault and we are doing all we can to find recovery. It is what it is and we are going to love and support ourselves with or without all these mental issues. So the first step is to know it was not your fault and you should not feel ashamed but feel proud of yourself.

Second step is to know you are not the only one. There are millions of people struggling with mental issues and maybe you can join a support group. How about a Facebook group with people that suffer with anxiety or whatever it is that you suffer with? Go ahead and get out of the closet with strangers. That could be a very, very big step. Step three and very important is to know that you are not weak or less valuable because you mentally suffer.

ACTIVITY 23

In this chapter we are going to focus on our shame. Go ahead and meditate who told you that it was bad and weak to struggle with mental issues. Who gets to say that having cancer is ok but having depression is not? Who said that physical illness is ok, but emotional illness is only for the weak? Who ever said that, definitely had no clue what it is to suffer mentally. Do not be ashamed of anything you are struggling with. It was not your fault, period.

You cannot move forward to the next chapter about getting out of the closet with your struggles, until you deeply believe there is nothing wrong with you. Why? Because if there is nothing wrong with us, we will not even

SETTING MYSELF FREE FROM MY OWN MIND.

fear what others think of us. Remember, our outer life is a mirror of our inner life. The goal here is to not be ashamed of our struggles that we don't have to even hide them. To accept ourselves as we are and to deeply know that there is nothing wrong with us. In order to reprogram our mind with this new information, I am going to ask you to meditate and visualize yourself at the age the mental struggle/disorder began. You are going to re-parent your inner child/teen/adult in this area. You are going to tell her that none of this was her fault and how proud you are of her. Tell her she is not alone, you are with her, but also that many suffer like her. Tell her, it is kind of normal and expected due to her upbringing, and that it is going to be ok and get better. Tell her many have overcome issues like the one she is struggling with. But she needs to know there is nothing to be ashamed of. You also need to make sure she knows that there has never been anything wrong with her. She actually developed those coping mechanisms as a way of saving herself at that moment. Tell her she did her best and that you are so grateful. Tell her that those coping mechanisms are hurting her now and we are working on building new brain patterns that make us happy now. Tell her anything you think that might help. Do these until you see a smile in her face. Repeat to her that it was not her fault at all and there is nothing to be ashamed of.

When you get here; then it will be lots easier to come out of the closet (be real) and be set free of the fear of what we think others might think of us. Whoever leaves because we struggle, most likely, is because they struggle too and are afraid to confront their own fears. Move on and keep those who embraced you with or without struggles. Set yourself free.

What if our struggle (mental struggle) is not the actual problem? What if the real problem is the shame we feel about how we feel? It is sad that shame has been attached to mental problems for

SETTING MYSELF FREE FROM MY OWN MIND.

generations. The truth is that it was not our fault that we suffer or have suffered with mental issues.

SETTING MYSELF FREE FROM MY OWN MIND.

24 VULNERABILITY

Brené Brown says something like this: "Either you do vulnerability or vulnerability does you". In other words, either you take the risk to show the real you and maybe lose the relationship, or the real you will show up and ruin the relationship. That is my understanding. Please take the time to watch her YouTube videos or buy her books. Time well spent.

KEEPING SECRETS KILLS FROM THE INSIDE OUT.

In the show/auto biography "Special" on Netflix - Ryan shows himself as gay, which he is. He apparently has no issues sharing with the world that he was gay. Proud of him. But he also has cerebral palsy and he is very afraid of what others might think if they knew the truth. He created a story about a car accident. He finally comes out of the closet with his cerebral palsy towards the end of the show. This made such an impact in my life! How many things am I hiding from others? Secrets kill us. I follow Ryan on Instagram, it is just amazing to watch how he openly talks about all the energy he wasted on keeping a secret and trying to please others. Love him to pieces. He is so real.

After being on your side 24/7 it will not be so hard to present yourself real, as you are, without any masks. The good news is that, by this point, we really do not care that much who leaves and who stays after the real us is out. Real people attract real people. You will begin attracting healthier relationships. Life is lived a thousand times better this way, feelings rock. Being willing to be vulnerable up front ends fake relationships. And that is good news. Just be courageous and be. This does not

SETTING MYSELF FREE FROM MY OWN MIND.

mean we have to go tell everyone we meet about our struggles with depression or anxiety, or anything else we struggle with. Not everyone deserves your story. But be true to yourself in all your actions, most likely words won't even be necessary afterwards.

ACTIVITY 24

Meditate on: what are the secrets that continue to keep you in bondage. Pick the biggest one and share with someone you trust. Whatever that might be: "Your son is gay. You are addicted to pills. You wake up in the middle of the night and eat. You throw up after you eat. You drink two bottles of wine a night. You have terrible feelings towards some. You stole money before. You have a sexual addiction, etc." and observe what happens next. Watch some leave and watch some stay. Be real, set yourself free. We all need support and keeping it a secret is for sure not helping.

Do not be so hard to yourself and be PROUD. You are working on it and it is getting better and better. Choose to love yourself today **as you are**. You do not have to wait until you get better to love yourself or it won't happen. It is the love from you to you that will deeply heal you. Yes, addictions are terrible, but keeping them inside is not helping. Chances are people around you either know it, or have big suspicions about it. Let us see who leaves and who stays to help and support you. Remember, whatever you are struggling with, it was not your fault, period! If you have read by now, you now know this is the result of brain patterns formed at early age and we had no clue of what was going on. We are taking full responsibility of them now and working on loving ourselves, honor yourself. Be proud.

SETTING MYSELF FREE FROM MY OWN MIND.

25 FOCUSING ON THE POSITIVE AND BEING THANKFUL

It is sad that we are usually waiting for the other shoe to drop. We focus on the one airplane crash and never take the time to focus on the thousands of daily flights that land safely.

"Waiting for the other shoe to drop" is an expression about a person awakened by a neighbor who loudly dropped one shoe on the floor and is waiting for the second shoe to be dropped. [Early 1900s]

I do not know exactly why this happens, but our brain likes to focus on the negatives and not so much on the positives. Maybe because the negatives have a chance of danger and we need to be alerted to do something about it. The truth is I do not know, I am not spending my time finding out why we sometimes think negatively. Remember, I am not here to blame but to change and correct our thinking that will eventually lead us to an effortless life of joy and peace. What I do know is that if we continue to focus on the fear, we are holding on to pain. We are holding on to a low vibe thought and therefore feeling, so we continue to auto destroy or hurt ourselves.

To be able to break this pattern we are going to have to consciously focus on our thoughts and then learn to switch our mentality: from negativity to positivity.

First of all, we need to accept that we definitely live in a world that is not utopia/perfect. We need to accept that it is what it is; and sometimes there is nothing we can do about it. With this said, yes, the other shoe might eventually drop, or it may never drop. I am suggesting to

SETTING MYSELF FREE FROM MY OWN MIND.

make a conscious decision that if it ever drops we are going to deal with it then –but for now- we are going to focus on enjoying life. We manifest what we focus on. I am choosing to focus on all the things that daily go well instead of on all that go wrong or could potentially go wrong.

Imagine we fear that one of our children could get sick. And then, the child does get sick at age 16 and we then dealt with it. What happened is that we lived in fear for 16 years, creating nonproductive fear and anxiety in our lives. Imagine what this anxiety is doing to your immune system on a daily basis. Not only your child did not get sick for 16 years, you didn't enjoy life.

Have you, for one day, ever focused on every single thing that goes –or went- well? Oh yes, we missed our flight and we are so angry. But did you focus on every single organ and cell of your body working properly? Have you ever focused on your air conditioner, water heater, refrigerator, working properly for years all the time? Have you ever focused on the car that takes you to work and works properly every day? See my point?

Why not live with a grateful heart? Studies have proved that having a life of gratitude changes it all. Isn't this what prayer should be? Can we focus on all those that love us and every single thing that goes well on a daily basis? Imagine what this could do to our lives and our immune system too.

ACTIVITY 25

Search the internet and find videos, audio books, or books to learn about gratitude. Begin to make a list of things you are grateful for. For seven days daily add 3-4 big things you are grateful for. Then begin writing about all the small details on your daily life that go well. How

SETTING MYSELF FREE FROM MY OWN MIND.

about your heart, are you grateful to your heart that it works properly every single day? Admit that the other shoe might eventually drop but we are going to handle it when it drops, if it ever drops. We are not going to fear for it. We are going to enjoy life, and be consciously happy with who we are and what we have today. Consciously focus on the good

Did you know that it is ok not to be ok?

SETTING MYSELF FREE FROM MY OWN MIND.

26 IRRATIONAL FEARS

What is the difference between fear and irrational fear or phobia? Fear is a feeling, therefore a messenger and it's a good one to have. Fear might keep us safe in many situations or dangerous circumstances. The problem begins when the fear is unfounded and is now affecting our life due to high levels of anxiety. An irrational fear is when we fear something that really does not present real or actual danger to us but produces high levels of anxiety so we end up avoiding those circumstances at all costs. Examples of these irrational fears might be: fear of flying, closed places, driving on the highway, spiders, dentists, etc.

The reason why irrational fears control us is because there is some truth attached to them. Take the fear of flying. Yes, you can die in a plane crash. That is a fact, but basically a fact or half-truth that is missing crucial information. The complete truth would include a little more information than that. How often do plane crashes happen? How many flights make it safe on a daily basis? What are the possibilities that this might happen to me? For these answers we would have to do an extensive search and then take a better informed decision about flying or not.

The problem I see here is that most likely these phobias began at an early age where nobody explained us the other half of the fact or truth. So if a child saw a plane crash on the news and no one explained that this rarely happens, this child's brain would have made connections to some information that was not a 100% truth. The child would deeply believe that planes crash without any questioning. And now, as an adult, the child has no clue why he gets

SETTING MYSELF FREE FROM MY OWN MIND.

panic attacks every time he even thinks of flying. To make matters worse, this adult now is feeling tremendous shame because he can clearly see that all of his friends fly on a regular basis, without any fear at all. And the cycle continues. Once we believe a half-truth as a fact in our subconscious mind, our entire body reacts to this half-truth as if it was totally literal truth. So then, we try to be courageous and we get on a plane after taking a Xanax, or end up having a panic attack up there, since our body is effortlessly reacting to what we believe to be true. All our brain and body are doing is reacting to the lie (half-truth) we deeply believe.

I totally believe that a big part of the healing process is to confront our fears. No way around it, but I do think that it is 100% easier when we finally discover the lie (half-truth) we deeply believe and replace it with a fact that is closer to the truth. Remember, the truth will always set us free. We will never be able to get rid of the irrational fear and consequences until we take the time and search what the lie (half-truth) is we deeply believe, that is now causing us so many problems.

I am not against medications; I have taken Xanax many, many times to be able to deal with my very real fears that were founded on very irrational lies (half-truths) I used to believe. So do not add any shame to yourself if you have to take meds while you search for the truth that eventually will set you free.

I believe that understanding this will be the very first step to overcoming an irrational fear or phobia. Another thing I want you to know is that this is more common than you think; only people do not go on talking about their deepest fears in fear of sounding like a failure.

ACTIVITY 26

SETTING MYSELF FREE FROM MY OWN MIND.

I want you to meditate and figure out if there are any irrational fears you deeply believe and are now creating a problem in your life. Most people have phobias against spiders and snakes. Those irrational fears rarely create a problem in our lives. We just do not go to wooded walks and the problems were solved. But what happens if the irrational fear is really causing you big problems and shame? What about you work ten minutes away from home but the drive includes a bridge? The problem is you are irrationally afraid of heights and you end up driving 30 extra minutes twice a day to be able to avoid driving on the bridge. Now that would definitely be a problem.

What I want you to do this week is, to find out if there is an irrational fear that is worth your time this week. If the answer is yes, I want you to write your irrational fear or phobia on a piece of paper.

Then I want you to write down all the facts that you deeply believe about it. I honestly know that this will create anxiety. Just breathe and trust me on this. Do it.

I then want you to go to the internet, in spite of the tremendous anxiety you must be feeling now, and search the complete facts of the circumstance. I want you to type this newly found info and read it to yourself at least twice a day. I want you to read it right before you go to bed and right after you wake up in the morning.

Once you feel a little more comfortable doing this, I want you to reach the altered state of the mind and visualize (imagine) yourself being victorious doing the very thing that used to cause you anxiety. See it in your mind happening and check your anxiety levels. Baby steps are ok.

Once you can visualize it in your mind without any major anxiety attack, I want you to be begin confronting your fears in real life. Example: someone with irrational fears of dogs will begin by watching pictures of dogs. Then going to a park where she or he might encounter some leashed dogs, etc. Someone with social phobia

SETTING MYSELF FREE FROM MY OWN MIND.

might begin by watching pictures of family birthday parties. Then go ahead and attend one, while knowing that she or he can leave at any moment without any explanations. Driving in her/his own car is a great idea at this point, etc.

Let's us work on our fears and get rid of them once and for all. There are many methods that I have used to reprogram my subconscious mind to remove the lie and replace it with the truth that set me free. We manifest what is recorded in our subconscious mind whether we like it or not, so the victory will come to us effortlessly once the lie is replaced with the complete truth or fact.

I do not claim any of these methods to be mine, except the Utopia meditations created for this book. The rest, I learned them all by either attending classes, guided by an instructor, reading or watching videos; but I did practice them all.

I have used: TAT – Tapas acupressure technique, EFT or tapping, REM visualization, EMDR, self-hypnosis and some other ways. I have meditated for years and I found it extremely helpful. I have made YouTube videos about how I use them all, in order to help more. So feel free to search on my YouTube channel and have fun finding out which one you like best.

As time goes by and we continue to work on finding the lies we believe, it gets easier and we will eventually conclude that "anxiety" is and never was the real enemy. The real enemy is our belief system and wrong thinking. All I can say is that if I feel anxiety, I do not oppress it. I just know that it is my red flag that tells me somehow that I am departing from self-love and self-respect. That is my time to meditate and find out what I am believing, thinking and therefore doing wrong. Overwhelming peace follows. It is a process.

Do a search on line of all methods to reprogram your own subconscious mind and practice a few. What I have discovered after years of practice is that the subconscious

SETTING MYSELF FREE FROM MY OWN MIND.

mind gets reprogrammed with emotions and feelings faster than with words and mantras. I spend time visualizing myself victoriously doing what I have been afraid to do for years. The feelings follow; feelings of joy and peace. I do this, before falling asleep and right after I wake up in the mornings. We can definitely reprogram our subconscious mind. I sometimes use music for meditation but not always, do what is best for you.

I wonder how many people are afraid of swimming at the beach after watching the movie "Jaws" as a child.

SETTING MYSELF FREE FROM MY OWN MIND.

27 DO WE EVER FULLY RECOVER OR DO WE JUST MANAGE IT?

Why the setbacks? Our brain was mainly wired by the age of five. Strong connections of self-destruction (coping mechanisms) were made back then and have been made even stronger as the years went by. I believe that once we overcome, it becomes easier and easier, but that does not always mean we cannot have setbacks.

If we are serious about our emotional health, and we truly made it this far and committed to the path of radical self-love and self-respect, most of the anxiety (and depression) has already disappeared on its own. Only a few triggers will put us back in the self-destructive path, therefore the importance of catching the anxiety and the depression in the first few stages.

How to get rid of anxiety and depression that want to continue to come back? The problem with anxiety/depression is that it comes attached with a few more fears of its own. We basically have three fears. We are afraid of the anxiety itself, the fear of happening again, and the fear of what others would think if they knew we suffer from anxiety.

I am going to focus a lot more on anxiety than on depression, because my struggle has been mostly with anxiety; but I believe that they usually come together. Most people usually struggle with both.

I have learned that we need to face all fears attached to the actual anxiety so it does not come back often. We first need to remember that there is nothing wrong with us. Usually the anxiety has a reason to be there as explained in past chapters.

SETTING MYSELF FREE FROM MY OWN MIND.

Second we need to know that, although panic attacks and anxiety are very scary and horrible, no one has ever died of the actual panic attack. Many end up in the emergency room only to find out that it was not an actual heart attack. But I think we really need to admit and acknowledge that it feels horrible. (Many experience anxiety with similar symptoms of a heart attack.) This is what I have learned and has worked for me in the past. While the anxiety attack is happening, I do not oppress it but acknowledge it feels terrible. By now I know it is temporary and will eventually get better.

I consider that I have totally recovered from anxiety and panic attacks (the last two panic attacks were six years apart) but as soon as it happens (a setback or a trigger), it is usually a result of stored stressed and tiredness. Knowing this I do my best to exercise often, to focus on my feelings and act accordingly at all times.

As mentioned before, I do not have anything against medications; I have taken them at some point in my life. But I do all my best to take herbs and vitamins to lower my stress levels on a daily basis, so I can use medication while the actual panic attack is happening. It seems to work better. Once the actual panic attack is happening, I take my med and then focus on my breathing. I breathe in for two and then breathe out for four. If that does not help I begin counting backwards from a 100, by threes or fours, something difficult so that I really have to think about it.

After the episode is gone, I would have to work on serious meditating, to try and figure out what it is that I still believe that is not necessarily true, or what it is that I am doing, causing my anxiety. Either way, while the panic attack is going full force, just focus on feeling better and know it will not kill you, and it is definitely temporary.

The second fear is the fear of the anxiety/panic attack coming back. After the episode is gone, I then try to repeat the trigger as soon as possible. I try to put myself

SETTING MYSELF FREE FROM MY OWN MIND.

in the same situation that triggered it and act differently. (After I meditated and I worked on removing the lie from my subconscious mind).

If we, on the contrary, try to remove ourselves from the trigger, the fear will eventually grow and we will be missing on life. Living in fear is no fun at all, it is just surviving, and it is not living. Spend some time facing your triggers and know that anxiety won't kill you. Remember, anxiety is the messenger. Confront your fears while you are still working with your belief system in relationship to your triggers. If your fear is traveling, travel. If you fear is big parties: go to one, but make sure you have already worked on what went wrong the last time so you can fix your thinking and acting. Baby steps, in my opinion, are the trick. Break the pattern in your mind ASAP; anything you resist - persists.

Then I focus on fear number three: the fear of others watching me during a panic attack and seeing the symptoms. First of all I would not tell the entire world about your fears. Your story is precious and only those you can rely on can be trusted with your deepest struggles. If, while you are facing fear two in front of people and the anxiety or panic attack comes, just breathe and say something like – "I am experiencing some anxiety; I think I need to leave". You do not have to explain a lot. All I am saying is "don't hide it". The amount of people not telling you they (also) suffer from anxiety and depression will surprise you. Anything you hide grows.

It is what it is, it was not your fault you are suffering from PTSD. Nobody chooses to have anxiety and depression. In my opinion anxiety and depression are not even our enemies. They are here as messengers to let us know something we believe and think is totally not true.
The sooner you welcome them and begin dealing with what they are trying to show you, the sooner you will get healed.

Once you know what the deep issue, trauma or lie -

causing your anxiety- is, you can work on it. In my case the fear of failing was big. I grew up with a mother that did not approve of me. I tried to be perfect so she would like me. The patterns of perfectionism were set in my brain at an early age. So I had to go even deeper to find out the lie I deeply believed about myself. It was not that I had to be perfect to be loved. The deeper lie was that I thought I was not ok the way I was, a human. I then had to go back to my inner child and assure her she was ok the way she was and I was always going to approve of her.

I suggest you never ever stay in bed in regards to depression. Always continue to be active while we search our heart for the real root of the depression. Never go to bed and stay in the fetal position, our body position matters. Our posture can change the chemicals in our minds and body. Never go to fetal position when having anxiety and/or depression. Go to superhero or victory position for two minutes and breathe in light. Watch how peace comes back. A straight back does wonders for the energy in our body. Stand up and stay in the super hero position for about two minutes then one more minute in the victory position, visualizing you overcoming this depression.

ACTIVITY 27

Face your triggers. Based on all new information learned here, make a written plan on facing all your triggers. Meditate on the lies we deeply believe that are hidden, now causing anxiety and/or depression in our lives. Ask for professional help if you need it. No shame about asking for help please. Remember it is always a process.

SETTING MYSELF FREE FROM MY OWN MIND.

28 UTOPIA MEDITATION
AGES 22-33 EARLY ADULT

HEART CHACKRA – UNBALANCED: WHEN WE STRUGGLE WITH LOVING OURSELVES.

Although the solar plexus chakra is very important and powerful, the heart chakra is the most important of all, because -if we have not loved- we have not accomplished much. It is here that we decide to love ourselves unconditionally after having received the revelation of who we really are. This requires a level of maturity on our part; therefore this chakra becomes awakened around age 22-33.

Day after day we claim we love ourselves, but we rarely do. If we could listen to our inner talk, it would reveal the truth about our love for ourselves. This is the chakra where we find the beginning of the love story. Jesus is represented in the Bible as the Love chakra and He began to show us our real and true nature: LOVE. The Heart chakra is the middle chakra and connects the three lower chakras or physical chakras with the three higher chakras or spiritual chakras. It is here, through the LOVE chakra that the physical and the spiritual realms become ONE. It is here that the two dimensions merge. It is through a balanced heart chakra that other chakras align and begin to work properly physically, emotionally and spiritually.

When we finally begin to love ourselves, then and only then, we are able to begin to love others. When we love ourselves, when love is the driving force behind all our emotions and actions, carnal pleasures begin to serve us, instead of us being controlled by them. This is where we become the master of our lives and leave the victim mentality, trusting that our motives are pure and kind, since our true nature is LOVE.

This is where we get out of the prison. The Love chakra is the door to freedom. This is where all those carnal pleasures become our blessings and all of our actions are driven by love. This is where all desires for carnal pleasures stop controlling us. Love never fails; it is the only path to heaven on earth and to the enlightenment of the next three spiritual chakras. This is where ALL the power for healing comes: LOVE. Love never fails! When the Love chakra is awakened and balanced we become free at last!

ACTIVITY 28

INSTRUCTIONS FOR ALL UTOPIA MEDITATIONS. (Skip if you already know what you are doing.)

We are going to stand up this time, which will help us to not fall asleep. We are going to spread our feet a little bit to maintain balance because I am going to ask you to close your eyes. So close your eyes and begin deep breathing. With each breath we are going to see light in and darkness out. At this moment we do not need to know what it is that we are exhaling. Just know that any low vibe energy that does not help you to be happy and healthy will now leave. Just trust the process and feel like you are inhaling life and exhaling death. Breathe in light, exhale darkness. Breathe in high vibe and exhale low vibe. As you are doing this I want you to see this light entering from your head and going all the way to the bottom of your spine and turning around up creating a big oval. As you do these, with your eyes closed, roll your eyes backwards. (This is a hypnosis tool.) Do these as long as you need and let it all go.

Begin focusing on your face, relax your forehead and then relax your jaw. Move to your neck and shoulders and consciously relax them. Repeat all this until you end up relaxing your toes. Take your

SETTING MYSELF FREE FROM MY OWN MIND.

time and do not continue until you believe you are as relaxed as you are going to get.

Once you are there, begin focusing on the next area up from your spine in the heart area, and see the color "green".

You are going to visualize yourself at that age span, being so at peace with your being and feeling completely comfortable in your skin. You will see yourself with a big smile on your face. You will visualize yourself being so connected within and in touch with all your emotions, feelings and desires. You see yourself taking all decisions based on what you feel and hear within. You are so connected that finally your authenticity feels good and flows effortlessly. You also see yourself, not depending on others or circumstances to feel at peace. You see yourself as a whole individual that meets all your emotional needs on a daily basis.

Now I want you to visualize yourself allowing only healthy and respectful relationships and feeling OK with all those relationships that you chose not to continue. You see all your self-esteem coming from being, not from doing, having or looking a certain way. You just are happy with who you are. You see yourself experiencing the highest vibration of love, your heart.

Continue to watch yourself effortlessly attracting healthy relationships and attracting those who are whole and not dependent individuals. You have no need of being a victim or a martyr, you are whole and have power to make decisions and changes that please and serve you.

See yourself enjoying pleasure and not feeling guilty or ashamed. See yourself being compassionate and empathic with yourself and as a result with those around you. See yourself being your own best friend and always on your best interest at heart. You are your own encourager and supporter. See yourself connected to your heart and honoring all your feelings at all times, see how this produces effortless love and joy. See yourself being authentic at all times and having no need of wearing masks so that others like you, because you like yourself the way you are. See yourself not controlling anything or anyone around you. You feel and act accordingly based on what is best for you.

You let go of other's opinions and others trying to manipulate you. Feel the peace and joy coming to you at all times. See yourself falling asleep at peace every night. Pay attention to the lack of depression and anxiety. See yourself smiling when you go to bed and smiling when you wake up in the morning. Experience effortless peace and joy, feel it. We finally ended the search. We found ourselves, the real treasure. No lack.

Finish your meditation when you are ready, come back to it as many times as needed until you feel totally comfortable and the new story coming easily to your mind, like it really happened. End your meditation with the light in your spine and open your eyes when you are ready. Do this meditation three times a day for at least seven days.

You can make these affirmations too: "I matter. My feelings matter. I am important. My feelings point me at the path of self-loving and self-healing. I am compassionate and feel empathy towards myself. I am whole. I have no lack. My perceptions about myself matter. I am worthy. There is nothing wrong with me. I love myself unconditionally. I do not judge myself. I accept myself. I forgive myself. I am not hard on myself. I have all wisdom inside. I am connected with my being. I do not need to wear masks for others to like me. I show the real me, good friends will stay as a result of my healthy relationship with myself. I will only accept healthy relationships. I do not judge others. I let others be. I am complete and lack nothing". Whatever works for you is perfect!

SETTING MYSELF FREE FROM MY OWN MIND.

The result of this aligned heart chakra is:

- Emotional well being
- Effortless joy and peace
- Have wisdom to take decisions
- Feel free to feel
- Honor feelings
- Honor ourselves
- We stop judging ourselves and others
- Healthy relationships
- Compassion and empathy
- Love overflowing

Our portal to higher dimensions is our heart.

SETTING MYSELF FREE FROM MY OWN MIND.

29 CAN YOU SAY "NO" AND NOT FEEL GUILTY?

The goal of this week is to learn to be assertive and use our voice to stand up for ourselves and/or anything we believe in. I believe that many of us fear being assertive and freely expressing what we feel, in fear of what others might think, or that it could make others feel uncomfortable. If we just did our job, as we have learned in the past chapters, to put ourselves first -or equal to others- that probably already brought some peace into your life. The problem here is that if we do not learn to respectfully speak up -and ask for what we need and want- we will not move forward with our healing.

Many of us were so afraid to lose approval from others that we not only oppressed our feelings but our voice too, allowing others to walk all over us. We have been doing some growing for now, we are more in touch with our feelings, and this is the time when our voice will have to match our feelings and actions. We are the ones that set the stage for others to respect us and I find it very hard for this to happen if we do not use our voice properly.

Early low self-esteem had two ways of manifesting in regards to our speaking. Either we learned to speak loud and manipulate conversations in order to manipulate people and circumstances so we could use them to fill our needs, or we became quiet and allowed all to walk all over us and be used. In other words we became the narcissist or the codependent the narcissist uses.

By now we hopefully removed ourselves from all toxic relationships or all relationships that didn't make us feel well. I am thinking that many of your old friends still have no clue what happened to you. But it is now that we will begin working on our assertiveness and set the stage for more respectful relationships. It is now that, by using our voice, we might allow some of our old friends to come back, but with a huge lot of clear, new set boundaries. We couldn't let others know what we expect and want, if we were not using our voice. Our voice will begin to match our newly found self-love. We will begin to make sense to others. Do not be surprised if some are beginning to ask what you are doing and will get interested in joining you.

Being assertive means saying "no" when we mean "no", and "yes" when we mean "yes", without any fear of what others will feel or think. We know what we want and we speak what we want and is best for us.

Gabor Maté says something like this: "If you do not learn to say 'no', your body will say 'no' ". In other words, if you do not learn to say "no", your body will say "no" loud and clear and you will affect your immune system. Not to mention that anxiety will remain.

ACTIVITY 29

First of all I want you to meditate on how you are using -or not using- your voice in your favor. I want you to meditate on how this is affecting your life if you are so afraid to be assertive and confronting. Who pays the price for you not speaking up in a respectful way?

I also want you to not be so hard on yourself. Hardly any of us had a model of what being respectfully assertive and setting healthy boundaries is. How many of us believed a teacher gave us a wrong grade and we decided to ignore it, due to fear of confrontation with someone with more power than us? How many of us spoke behind someone else's back instead of going to talk to that person

SETTING MYSELF FREE FROM MY OWN MIND.

directly and explain why we felt the way we felt? How many of us think we needed a raise and were so afraid to go talk to our boss about it? I think you get my point by now.

This is a huge epidemic. I hardly know very many assertive people that are not afraid to confront abuse. The question to ask ourselves will be: "Why do we take the abuse"? Well, if we decided to radically love ourselves, due to being tired of experiencing anxiety and depression, the question I am now going to ask you is, "How serious are you about healing"? Because healing will require for you to act according to self-love and that will require lots of boundaries and speaking up loud and clear. I am asking you not to be so hard on yourself and take baby steps.

How about we begin to say "No, thank you", on a text? Then we practice lots in front of a mirror until we are ready to do it face to face. If saying "no" is still too hard for you, practice saying: "let me think about it". This will buy you time, so you get courageous enough to say, "I am truly sorry but I can't go with you to _____, maybe another time."

Please do not over explain, most people do not care. Do not feel the need to explain if you do not have to. You have every right to be an individual with a mind and heart being able to decide for yourself. Now be assertive.

This week I want you to begin to be assertive in little things. I am going to ask you to be assertive in one big thing too, something that has been bothering you for maybe even years. Maybe a friend that mistreated you years ago and you want to be able to let her know a few things. Do it. Maybe to a coworker who has been using you for years and you finally will be able to say, "I am sorry, I can't help you this week".

Once you learn and experience the joy and peace that will effortlessly come to you, you will continue in this path. Remember, this is a process. We are in the process of changing our belief system about our worth. Then our

SETTING MYSELF FREE FROM MY OWN MIND.

actions needed to match our new found self-worth and now our words have to match too. It is going to feel good. Enjoy.

One minute of courage, can lead to a life of joy.

SETTING MYSELF FREE FROM MY OWN MIND.

30 HEALTHY COMMUNICATIONS

Being assertive will take a while to learn, but the more we do it, the easier it will get. It is definitely a process. This week we are going to help ourselves be done with the fear of communicating our feelings by doing all sorts of activities.

ACTIVITY 30

Get a journal and write. Remember, no one else will read it. Write about your fears, your dreams or whatever it is you are thinking of now. I want you to write about your feelings on a daily basis. How do I feel, why do I feel this way, and what do I need to change about my perceptions in relationship to this feeling, what can I do? Finally, what can I say (and who to) about it? This activity will help us with creativity and allowing ourselves to be in touch with our feelings and communicate more. We have to start at some point, right?

I also want you to begin to sing. For some of us that sing horribly, don't worry, set yourself free and sing in your car on your way to work. Imagine you are right there with the singer and you both are singing together. Imagine people watching you and applauding you for singing. Who cares how you sing. This will help your subconscious mind to look at you speaking under a different light. This will remove so many fears and blocks. Sing and dance if possible.

I want you to begin expressing your feelings towards others. If someone did something nice to you, I want you to write a thank you note (or send a text message) and thank that person. Tell him why it made you feel special. Make an effort to at least write a few sentences.

If someone means the world to you, I want you to begin saying it not only with actions but with words. Express your feelings towards others. If someone hurt your feelings, I want you to be honest and talk to that person. If it is still too hard to do it in person: send a text message, it is always a good way to start.

Part of healing our voice and achieve healthy communication is to also learn to listen. Practice listening. Listen to what others have to say. Learning to respect ourselves eventually takes us to learn how to respect others. Listen attentively and think before you answer. It is totally OK to say, "I do not know, but I am here". Allow yourself to not know all the answers, just listen.

Watch a movie that makes you laugh. Laugh out loud without feeling guilty or conscious about it. Laugh a lot. How about a movie that makes you cry? Do it and cry a lot. Allow yourself to cry even for personal situations that you might still have trapped.

If you are dealing with anger, go ahead and find a place where you feel safe and scream. Then come back and be assertive about the situation. The screaming helps.

Spend time in silence; listen to your heart. Visualize in your mind how to properly assertively take care of yourself or the situation and then do it. There is always a respectful way to take care of ourselves. Do it.

SETTING MYSELF FREE FROM MY OWN MIND.

31 UTOPIA MEDITATION
THROAT CHAKRA BALANCED

THROAT CHAKRA – BALANCED: WHERE WE SPEAK WHAT WE HEAR WITHIN

It is from this chakra that we speak what is in our heart. If this chakra is out of balance we either don't stand up for ourselves, or we speak too much to cover up the low self-esteem. This chakra can reveal our thoughts. If we listen to our words, especially our inner words, or the way we talk to ourselves, they will reveal the level of our self-esteem. This is a very important chakra because our tongue has the power to heal or to hurt. This chakra cannot be balanced before our heart chakra is balanced; all that would come out of our mouth will be complaints. The way we talk to ourselves and to others reveals the condition of our heart.

When the heart chakra is balanced and we know who we are and we love and respect ourselves, we will no longer allow others to "walk all over us". Using the courage from the Solar Plexus we finally stop trying to be someone we are not, we take off the masks and accept our true selves. We begin to (respectfully) speak up and say what we think and feel, and finally stop caring what others think of us.

We start taking small steps toward confronting others who are hurting us, due to their ignorance or their own pain within. Confrontation is hard, but we can begin by sending emails or texts, until we learn to confront face to face.

This is a good time to grab a book about improving our

SETTING MYSELF FREE FROM MY OWN MIND.

communication skills. Since our throat chakra may have been blocked or unbalanced and not properly functioning, it is going to take a while for us to learn healthy patterns of communication.

ACTIVITY 31

INSTRUCTIONS FOR ALL UTOPIA MEDITATIONS. (Skip if you already know what you are doing.)

We are going to stand up this time, which will help us to not fall asleep. We are going to spread our feet a little bit to maintain balance because I am going to ask you to close your eyes. So close your eyes and begin deep breathing. With each breath we are going to see light in and darkness out. At this moment we do not need to know what it is that we are exhaling. Just know that any low vibe energy that does not help you to be happy and healthy will now leave. Just trust the process and feel like you are inhaling life and exhaling death. Breathe in light, exhale darkness. Breathe in high vibe and exhale low vibe. As you are doing this I want you to see this light entering from your head and going all the way to the bottom of your spine and turning around up creating a big oval. As you do these, with your eyes closed, roll your eyes backwards. (This is a hypnosis tool.) Do these as long as you need and let it all go.

Begin focusing on your face, relax your forehead and then relax your jaw. Move to your neck and shoulders and consciously relax them. Repeat all this until you end up relaxing your toes. Take your time and do not continue until you believe you are as relaxed as you are going to get.

Once you are there, begin focusing on the next area up, the area of your throat and see or visualize the color "blue". I want you to visualize (imagine) yourself at your actual age. Do not force the vision, let it come freely. Same as within past utopia activities -and with the help of our right hemisphere- we now are going to focus, create

SETTING MYSELF FREE FROM MY OWN MIND.

and imagine our perfect utopia life. We are going to see ourselves enveloped or surrounded in blue at all times.

I am going to ask for you to visualize yourself at your actual age with your mouth open and smiling. I want you to see yourself in this vision singing and enjoying singing. I want you to see yourself sharing with others about your feelings, and feeling comfortable about it. I want you to see yourself standing up for yourself and others in a very respectful way while you smile a lot. I want you to see yourself quiet in situations that normally will make you speak a lot if you were nervous, see yourself smiling and not saying a word. See yourself saying "yes" or "no" and meaning it. See yourself taking care of yourself at all times while you smile and have your back straight.

I want you to see yourself thinking before you answer. I want you to see yourself meditating and getting wisdom within and then acting and speaking accordingly. I want you to see yourself being assertive at all times. See yourself, confronting people with a smile. Ask the question of why such and such happened and then listen with a smile. See yourself making changes in your life due to happily being assertive and confronting any kind of oppression. I want you to see yourself, ending relationships with your voice. Not just disappearing without an explanation. I want you to see yourself singing and/or speaking in public and while doing so feeling totally comfortable in your skin and with a smile and good posture.

See yourself deciding what to share and what not to share with others. See yourself being so authentic that your words match your feelings and who you truly are. I want you to visualize yourself with healthy relationships due to healthy self-love and healthy communications, both speaking and listening. Finish your meditation when you are ready and come back to it as many times as needed as you feel totally comfortable and the new story coming easily to your mind like it really happened. End your meditation with the light in your spine and open your eyes when you are ready. Do this meditation three times a day for at least seven days.

You can make these affirmations too, "I matter, my feelings matter. I have no fear of expressing myself and my feelings. If others do not like me because I take care of myself - their loss. I respectfully speak my truth and expect others to respect me. I also respect others and I listen to their truth, it is OK to disagree. I use my words to create a life of love and respect. I express myself in a clear manner and full of confidence with a smile in my face and good posture. I honor my feelings and opinions, I speak up. I respectfully confront when I feel used or abused. I love myself and express what I feel I need to express. I set clear boundaries and follow them. I am comfortable with silence". Whatever works for you, is perfect!

SETTING MYSELF FREE FROM MY OWN MIND.

32 INTUITIONS

How intuitive are you? And do you follow your intuition? Think of your childhood, were you raised in a close minded family that free-thinking was not encouraged? Were you told what to believe but never allowed you to question those beliefs? Were you commanded to obey without any questioning? Did your parents encourage and value your insights? The answer to these questions will give you a good idea whether you are good at paying attention to your intuition and feelings or not.

Many call the third eye chakra as the doorway towards spiritual enlightenment. The third eye chakra is responsible for intuition, imagination, dreams, insight, and wisdom. It is located in the middle of our forehead and is usually associated with the pineal gland within our brain.

The pineal gland is responsible for sleep cycles and some hormones but many assure it has mystical attributes. Ancient cultures believed that this gland is responsible for spiritual awakening; the truth is we do not know. What I do know for sure and have experienced is the finding of higher truth within that sets me free in the blink of an eye. It is the wisdom within that we find during meditation that can set us free in an instant. We are now in chapter 32, so I am sure hoping that you are becoming such an expert at meditation and easily achieving the altered state of the mind.

For now we are going to focus on that hunch feeling or intuition that we all have experienced at some point in our lives. We are going to learn on how to allow ourselves to be more intuitive and to follow our gut feeling. We all

SETTING MYSELF FREE FROM MY OWN MIND.

have psychic abilities, we deep down know this because all of us have experienced intuitions or the feeling of "I just know it", at one time or another. Unfortunately many of us didn't pursue to grow our psychic abilities because we were taught to be afraid of them or that it did not come from god.

A person with a weak third eye chakra, or in other words, someone that didn't allow intuition to grow, is usually very good at overthinking and analyzing information. They find it hard to just not think and go with what the body is telling. How many times we go to an event where we somehow felt we shouldn't go, ending up feeling guilty for not paying attention to our inner voice? These people rarely recall their dreams and pay no attention to repetitive dreams. They also have a hard time setting their imagination free, therefore can't create a new life different from what they already have experienced. They also have a very hard time making decisions based on emotions, so they end up with a mind led life and continue to struggle since they are not balancing both hemispheres of the brain. A healthy life is achieved when we have both hemispheres balanced, where both the emotions/heart and mind matter. Needless to say, these are the people that had a strong disassociation of heart and mind. It is also said that these individuals usually have mental fog or get tired of thinking, causing headaches and sometimes depression.

Intuitive people or persons with a strong third eye chakra have a clear understanding of their purpose in life. Have an overall feeling of wholeness. They know thinking and analyzing is good but decisions are also taken based on their heart and what makes them happy. They do not make important decisions without seeking for wisdom or higher truth within. They pay close attention to their feelings and recognize them as the red flag when separating or walking away from truth. They pay close attention to their intuition and sometimes go with it

SETTING MYSELF FREE FROM MY OWN MIND.

without giving it any thought, and end up finding out that it was the right decision for them. They know their body does not lie and go with it. They are rarely influenced by others' opinions and beliefs. They respect themselves and others and allow themselves to respectfully disagree. These people are usually very open minded, not afraid to learn new things. They are also not afraid to question their own belief system if it is not working. These people are very sensitive and easily able to achieve the altered state of the mind or meditative state. These people usually use a "lingo" that might sound "woo-woo" and scare many. The truth is that, if you are not intuitive, you have no clue what they are talking about. They talk about higher dimensions, auras and synchronicity. So let us try not to judge, open our minds and learn.

The truth is nobody can help you to be intuitive; it is a gift we all have but few have been allowed the opportunity to grow this gift. What I know for sure is that a life with intuition, insight, imagination and wisdom is way more fun and easier than a life led exclusively by the mind. I have done both and I can testify to that.

This should be good news to all, because we do not need to pay a guru to come and help us. We do not need to pay a tarot card reader; all wisdom and higher truth for our entire life is free and within. It is very unfortunate that in the western countries most were not taught to search within and meditate. Blessed are those who were taught to meditate and go within, in search of their own heart at an early age.

ACTIVITY 32

In this chapter I want you to spend time finding all information you want about the third eye chakra, intuition and sixth sense (they call it sixth sense, due to the third eye chakra being the sixth chakra). The internet has lots of information and techniques, find what works for you. Find out about removing fluoride from your diet and what food and herbs to eat for making your third eye chakra stronger.

I wrote about the third eye chakra in my book "Levels of Awakening". This is what I had to say.

When we achieve a balanced third eye chakra, we begin to have visions with our inner eye during our meditations. There is an amazing bliss that comes at this stage, a drunkenness or light headed feeling. You can stay here as long as you want. It is here where the answers to all our questions come to us, either in thought form or in a vision. It is here where most of my emotional issues were resolved. Time flies here, so it could feel like minutes only to open your eyes and find out you were gone in the spiritual dimension for about an hour or more. Allow the Spirit to guide you into what you need to see and hear.

This week I want you to pay close attention to your intuition and to act accordingly, and then share with others who will understand. Have fun.

I also want you to spend time in solitude and meditate without an agenda. Just go within and see what happens. My favorite is to imagine and visualize a man that knows it all and I spend time with him. I usually come back from my meditation with a piece of higher wisdom that basically changes my life. There are no limitations, you can visualize and imagine as you please. You can also make a search on the YouTube channel for guided meditations. What I now want you to focus on is learning to go within with a few questions or just for the fun of it and see what happens. There is no wrong or right, the main purpose of this exercise is to go within and not to control.

SETTING MYSELF FREE FROM MY OWN MIND.

33 OPENING THE MIND

Just because we do not know anything about it, or have not experienced it, means that it is not real. All I am asking you is to listen. Listen to those that talk about higher dimensions. What do you think higher dimensions are? Do not be scared and ask the hard questions.

A problem I see with rigid and close minded people is that they find it very hard to experience anything new and even listen to their own intuition. Somehow they are afraid of anything that contradicts their belief system. But just remember: not everything taught to us was the absolute truth. We, most likely, still believe a lot of lies if our life doesn't model a life of peace and joy. I find it amazing when I spend time with the young, next generation. They are usually a lot more open minded than their past generation and they have a lot to say. Just listen. Most of the youth I know are radically on the side of love and equality. Yes, that could be scary for us who grew up in religion. But my take is, if any theology and or religion judges and divides, it is not from spirit, it is from ego.

ACTIVITY 33

Read new books, watch TV shows that can expand your mind; documentaries are amazing. Experiment new activities outside of your comfort zone. Be very curious about different cultures, perspectives and ways of life. Listen to what minorities have to say and what they have experienced. Open your mind.

SETTING MYSELF FREE FROM MY OWN MIND.

I am not saying to just believe everything you hear. Follow the lead of your heart. I have been considered to be rebellious by many, in a way I am. But I am always on the side of radical love and equality. Any theology, no matter how many believe it, if it separates, "us and them", I do not receive. There are no chosen ones; we are all one and the same. All I want you to learn this week is that, just because we are afraid of the new, or do not understand the "lingo", means it is nonexistent. Open your mind and life to experience more than what just the mind has to offer. Explore your limiting beliefs.

SETTING MYSELF FREE FROM MY OWN MIND.

34 BECOME THE OBSERVER

Like I said before, no one can teach you to become intuitive and how to search for wisdom within. It is a job you are going to have to do on your own. You are going to have to spend little extra time in meditation, using different techniques until you find what works for you and be able to find the higher truth that sets you free in an instant. Let us try something different that might help us now.

ACTIVITY 34

I want you to get your journal out and for a week write about all your feelings and what you did according to those feelings. I want you to reflect on your thoughts and feelings more than usual. And also write what you did, how you reacted to those feelings and thoughts. Was that a feeling of fear? What did you do about it? Oppressed it?

Or did you go on meditating to try and find out why you felt this way? What do you usually do when this fear shows up? What did you do differently this time? Write it all down and then read it in the following days. Let new ideas come to you.

During this week I want you to become the observer of your feelings and thoughts. While experiencing fear, close your eyes and see yourself getting outside of your body and watch you being afraid. Become the observer. There you will learn that feelings are just feelings and are temporary. Remember, the feeling is just the messenger. What is the message of this feeling?

During this week I want you to learn, at a subconscious

SETTING MYSELF FREE FROM MY OWN MIND.

level, that although feelings are very important, they are just the messenger and we are not the feeling itself. I want you to learn to detach from the feeling. Do not forget to have fun while doing this.

SETTING MYSELF FREE FROM MY OWN MIND.

35 LIVING IN THE NOW

There is so much information out there about, "Living in the now" but in my opinion many are missing the point. "Living in the now" is not just breathing and living as if "now" is the only possible time ever. "Living in the now" is a lot more than that. To me, "Living in the now" means to live like there is no past or future ever, or living without time limitations at all.

Let me explain: everything we see -and don't see- is energy. Energy has no time limitations; there is no beginning or end for energy. Energy cannot even be created or destroyed and is omnipresent. Sounds a lot like the description of god, right?

Well, in my opinion, if we experienced trauma as a five year old and have not dealt with it, that low energy of unforgiveness and being powerless is still inside your body today, creating problems in your now. Example: let us say your father abandoned you when you were five. You then felt it was partly your fault because if he didn't stay, it was because there was something wrong with you. Although a lie, it felt true at that age and we made up our mind. Now we might not remember any of our thoughts at age five. But you, somehow, still feel the same way about yourself. You still feel not good enough and fear new relationships because you are afraid they are eventually going to know the truth about you and abandon you. So no matter how much you want to live in the now and be happy, your "now" has low vibrational energy that feels so familiar to you because you have had it since you were five years old.

Living in the now means going back in time, with the help of imagination and visualization and fix the trauma; letting go of the all lies creating low vibrational energy in

SETTING MYSELF FREE FROM MY OWN MIND.

you. Bringing the truth to the situation will allow your subconscious mind to be programmed with more information, closer to factual truth. In this case the truth is that your dad might have abandoned you because he had a problem with alcohol or something else. The truth is every child is amazing and worthy, and nobody deserved to be abandoned. No matter how hard you try, you will not be healed until all traumas are dealt with properly and we bring light/truth (higher vibrational truth/energy) to the situation. When you begin to work with your energy, your life will change for the good, especially as we let go of the low vibe energy that was effortlessly produced by past experiences and is still producing self-destructive patterns.

ACTIVITY 35

About time we begin working and dealing with deep past trauma. Although we have talked about this in past chapters and we have worked on some, I want you to meditate and continue to work with past trauma from an energy level point of view.

With the help of your third eye, I want you to visualize your body and see where you could have trapped emotions or energy blocks. I want you to see yourself as a powerful individual that can work at getting rid of this low vibe energy in your mind and body now.

This might be a good time to get out the "Emotion code" book again and work some more. Remember, it is all a process.

With the help of our intuition and third eye chakra we can enter into an altered state of the mind and find out if we still have some unresolved trauma. Ask within if there are things that happened to you that you do not even remember? There is no right or wrong, just know that the path to complete healing is always within.

SETTING MYSELF FREE FROM MY OWN MIND.

36 ARE WE ALL PSYCHIC? DO WE ALL HAVE INTUITION? CAN WE TRUST OUR INTUITION?

It is hard for me to teach or even share how to open the sixth chakra. It is a job that has to be done by you. No one can teach you how to listen and pay attention to your intuition but YOU. Once we learn to listen and pay attention to our intuition, it will continue to be an ongoing process of learning how to live by our sixth sense and ignore what the other five senses are telling us. I am not saying we totally ignore our mind or our five other senses, I just want you to know that there is a lot more we can experience and a lot of wisdom within we could live by, on a daily basis. How many times has it happened to you that you ended up in a bad situation and the first words to yourself are, "I knew it, I knew I should have not come, or done this. Why did I not follow my intuition?"

It has been told that in the 2004 tsunami, the animals and native tribes of Sri Lanka went to higher ground before the big waves struck land. These people did not depend on their five senses or even technology to know that something was coming. The animals went to higher ground before the big wave. Are they any different than we are? Or are we just not trained and/or encouraged to follow our intuition or sixth sense? We have all heard stories of many people that claim to have psychic abilities. Do we all have them? Can we all develop them to help us achieve a more victorious life? I believe we do and this will change our lives.

SETTING MYSELF FREE FROM MY OWN MIND.

As mentioned before I cannot really teach anyone how to develop their intuition. In this chapter I will write about a few ideas of things you can do. But ultimately it is your desire to develop your sixth sense and use it for your own good and those around you, that will eventually make it manifest in your life.

ACTIVITY 36

I suggest that you do a search on the internet and spend some time reading and/or watching documentaries about people that use their psychic abilities for the good of their communities. There are documentaries about how even the police use people with psychic abilities to solve crimes, sometimes. This will definitely open your mind to the possibilities. This will also make you hungry for more, which in my opinion is what is needed now.

These are the activities that I can suggest here, but ultimately follow your heart and have fun. Do not expect your entire life to change in a few days. Small changes will be noticed in the first few days just by focusing within and not without.

- The very first activity I want you to do is to focus within and not without. Any struggle you have, I want you to quit focusing on circumstances and to focus on your feelings. I do this every morning and night, just to maintain focusing on my within – where the kingdom is. I want you to wake up and check your feelings. How do I feel about today? And ask yourself, why? Be totally honest. We are so trained to oppress our feelings that we totally do not pay attention to our feelings until they are very loud and sometimes painful. So stay connected with your heart at least three times a

SETTING MYSELF FREE FROM MY OWN MIND.

day. Repeat at night. Become your own best friend. It is within where peace and joy are found. Continue to practice at all times and go within.

- Before you go or make any decision, take a few minutes in a quiet place and check your intuition or "gut feeling". Then follow it. Record results in your journal.

- Pay attention to repetitive dreams, close your eyes and try to figure out what it all means to you.

- Check for repetitive situations, what are they telling you? What are we doing wrong?

- Before a long drive, keep a question in mind. While we keep our left hemisphere of our brain busy while driving, the right hemisphere will have a chance to download information. Never drive long distances without a question. If you are seeking a solution to a problem, ask within. It might take a while, but it will eventually come. Meditate and ask within.

- Feel the vibes. Train yourself to pay attention to the vibes you feel at all times. Go to a new grocery store and feel the vibes. Observe and feel the vibes when you meet new people. You will be able to remove yourself from places and people that carry a low vibe when you get good at this. Do not forget to pay close attention to your feelings in response to new places and people you may encounter on a daily basis.

- Stop brushing off the small quiet inner voice. It is ok to doubt it if we have never honored our inner voice. Take a chance, honor it and see what happens. Write it down if it helps you, then re-read to encourage you to do it more often.

- While meditating see a blue light coming from the center of your forehead, travelling around all your body. While meditating imagine and see yourself following your intuition and being successful. See yourself paying attention to all your feelings. Know that our struggles began in our mind and are resolved in our mind. Going within is always the path to healing, effortless joy and peace.

- Telepathy – try learning about it and have fun putting it into practice. Try communicating an important message to a friend that lives around the globe and see if she or he gets it. Have fun with this.

- Free writing – allow yourself to write what your inner voice tells you. This takes practice but it develops with time. Many like to write with their non-dominant hand to contact their inner child or heart.

- Try to read people's energy. You somehow know, without even asking, how they feel today; then ask and see how close you were. Or maybe you try reading the energy of people you do not know. See what comes to you. We are all psychic!

- Develop your imagination – stop judging yourself and feel free to imagine your best possible life. Focus on your feelings, stay with them, enjoy.

SETTING MYSELF FREE FROM MY OWN MIND.

- Star and moon gazing. Go outside at night and gaze at the stars. Do not forget the sun is a star too. Many claim that sun gazing is important. I only recommend watching a sunset. I also recommend lying down on the floor and with your eyes closed, to feel the rays of the sun entering your body through your third eye chakra and then going to all parts of your body. You can take it a little further and see this energy healing your body as it travels through it.

- Do a search on the internet and find other ways to open your third eye chakra. I recommend listening to guided meditations and music/sounds on YouTube videos. There is lots of free stuff on YouTube and the internet, just do a search for "eye chakra".

SETTING MYSELF FREE FROM MY OWN MIND.

SETTING MYSELF FREE FROM MY OWN MIND.

37 WHAT IS A HIGHER DIMENSION?

    While many could disagree with me, this is what I deeply believe and has helped me tremendously. When I was a Christian someone asked me: "Do you believe Jesus solved all of your problems at the cross? Do you believe he did make you a new creation and took all our sins away? Isn't this what Paul said? Did Paul not call you a "saint" at the beginning of all his letters? If you do believe, then why are you acting like he didn't do a thing? Why are you still praying and begging for something he did and he said it was finished? Are you a true believer or not?" These questions opened my mind, like nothing else. "Was I really a Christian?" I began asking myself.
    I have always known that we effortlessly manifest what we deeply believe. So this was a true awakening for me. I finally began to realize that it was me and my thinking creating most of my problems. I began to choose to believe that if he said it was finished, then it was. I began closing my eyes and imagine and see all of my problems/struggles solved in my favor and the favor of those around me. I began seeing myself as a happy person and giving love and joy to those around me. It did not take long to begin to experience peace in regards to some of my struggles. I am not saying that it manifested rapidly but I did have a change of mind. I began seeing all not as sinners but as people not knowing they were saints. If I needed a new job I began to see myself with a perfect job. If some of my loved ones were struggling with a specific area in their lives, I began seeing them with their problems solved. It did not take long for me to begin seeing all

SETTING MYSELF FREE FROM MY OWN MIND.

humanity as one humanity, in love with each other.

A huge part of overcoming any struggles is to deeply know we are not powerless and we have very many options. We can work with our energy and we can work towards creating a new outcome with our mind.

I began spending more and more time in a higher dimension. I began meditating morning and night and visualizing victory in all aspects of my life. My change of mind began to manifest effortlessly and with it, many blessed manifestations.

My understanding of this, has evolved even a little more. I believe in higher and lower dimensions. I believe we are here on earth manifesting what we deeply believe. A person that deeply believes he is worthy is not any different than you or me. He is just manifesting his state of the mind in a higher dimension than ours. He manifests blessings wherever he goes because he deeply knows and feels he deserves them. On the contrary, we are effortlessly manifesting struggle after struggle due to deeply believing a lie about ourselves. There are no blessed and unblessed humans. There are humans with different vibrational patterns of thinking or what many call, different dimensions.

With time, this way of thinking changed my life forever. I focused on the good and all my possibilities instead of all my struggles. I began to see I had options. I began to see that it was me who needed to change my mind and act on higher truth. I began connecting with people that were seeing through the eye of the heart and not the two physical eyes.

Did Jesus see the prostitute or did he see her heart? That is exactly when I began living by our higher reality and not the three dimension reality my five senses were seeing. Could it be we are all one spirit of love, only most do not know it? Souls do not have races, sexes or religions; those divisions only exist in and belong to our five senses and minds.

SETTING MYSELF FREE FROM MY OWN MIND.

ACTIVITY 37

Close your eyes and train your mind to spend at least 5-10 minutes daily on a higher dimension. See all of your struggles solved. See all your dreams coming to pass and feel the overwhelming joy. See yourself healed not only physically but emotionally as well. As time passes you will learn to effortlessly see life through your inner eye and not your physical eyes. This way of life effortlessly produces love, not only to yourself but to all you come in touch with. Enjoy learning about your higher truth. Once you begin to see your higher dimension as a real dimension of truth, you will begin to effortlessly manifest your higher true self. Achieve the spirit led life vs. the mind led life. Now this is what many call, "manifesting heaven on earth" – Spirit's will, done on earth as it is done in heaven.

SETTING MYSELF FREE FROM MY OWN MIND.

SETTING MYSELF FREE FROM MY OWN MIND.

38 LEARNING TO WORK WITH ENERGY

Dr. Bradley Nelson wrote "The Emotion code" -How to release your trapped emotions for abundant health, love and happiness. I have a YouTube video of how I practice it. But I strongly suggest you either buy the book or search for his information on line.

I now believe that what we used to call, "deliverance of evil spirits" in the church is really nothing more than working with low vibe energy. If you were abused by the age of five and have not solved this trauma in your mind and heart, these low vibe energies of resentment, anger and fear are still causing you problems in your life and body today. Remember, energy has no time limitations. Energy is always in the now or present time.

Dr. Nelson did an amazing job about teaching many of us how to get rid of these low vibe energy from our bodies and mind.

I still believe that what ultimately sets us free is not only the energy gone, but the change of mind that happens afterwards. If we happen to believe we are not good enough, this lie produces low vibes; not only in our body but in everything we do and touch. So, even if we remove the low vibe energy that is the result of our wrong thinking, nothing will change until we change our thinking.

All that is going to happen is that you are going to feel a little better now, but you eventually will feel the same or even worse, because of the loss of hope. It is my experience that after removing the low vibe energy, it somehow opens the way to a different way of seeing

SETTING MYSELF FREE FROM MY OWN MIND.

things. You will probably begin to have revelations and/or dreams that will eventually give you the "ah-ha" moment that we need to be set free. The truth in your mind is what eventually will set you free. In this case, the truth that your best is more than enough.

ACTIVITY 38

I want you to learn about "the Emotion code" and practice some. If you are afraid to try new things, just close your eyes and see your energy body, after you have achieved the altered state of the mind through meditation and deep breathing. I want you to see if, by using your intuition, you can see where you have stored low vibe or dark energy. Then, with the help of your imagination, I want you to see it leaving your body as you breathe out. You do not have to know what kind of low vibe is leaving your body.

If you want to go deeper, ask and see if your inner wisdom comes to you and lets you know what's continuing to produce all these low vibes inside. Do not be so hard on yourself, just imagine seeing it gone from your knees or wherever it is you saw it. If you did not see a thing, just "see", with the help of your imagination, all low vibe energy leaving your body. Then focus on the peace you will begin to effortlessly feel.

What I want you to do is to pay close attention to any revelation that might come to you in the near future after doing this exercise, even when you are not thinking about it. Most likely you will read something and it will click inside of you. You will have a few ah-ha moments. You will automatically say something like: "How come I never noticed this?" This is when the true deliverance happens, with the change of the mind, the new programming of our mind.

SETTING MYSELF FREE FROM MY OWN MIND.

I want you to become so good at this, that you can remove all resentment, anger and fear from the entire trauma experienced as a child. This can take weeks depending on how much you are still holding on to those feelings and thoughts. Just know that eventually, it is you who needs to set yourself free. We can't change the past or others; but we can always open our minds to the higher truth about ourselves. We are whole indeed!

SETTING MYSELF FREE FROM MY OWN MIND.

SETTING MYSELF FREE FROM MY OWN MIND.

39 UTOPIA MEDITATION
THIRD EYE CHAKRA BALANCED: WHEN WE SEE THE SPIRIT WITHIN

In the Throat chakra we learned how to be assertive in the physical world. But the main job of the three upper chakras is to connect with our Spirit. In the throat chakra we learned how we, through sound (tongues or mantras), can quiet the mind and begin to listen to Wisdom or Spirit. As we continue in meditation, we eventually begin to disconnect from earth, and the right side of the brain begins to kick in. At some point we begin to forget about the tongues and the mantras, this is where we begin to have visions. Our inner vision is contained here, inner dreams and clairvoyance happen here. This is where our Wisdom begins to flow effortlessly, in what is usually called a "revelation".

After a revelation from within, is where true repentance takes place, a change of mind. It effortlessly changes the way we think in an instant, or in the blink of an eye. We can never ever go back to the way we used to perceive things. This is where we finally begin to be set free from the lies we used to believe.

When we receive a revelation (truth that sets you free) and our thinking effortlessly changes, we see things that are now so obvious to us, but that most would not see or understand. Some might even think we have gone mad. Once we see, we can never be blind again. Once we have heard and seen the truth, our new mindset comes

SETTING MYSELF FREE FROM MY OWN MIND.

effortlessly, because after all, the higher truth not only uncovers the lies, but replaces them with the truth and sets us free. After we have tasted true freedom, no one can convince us to go back to the way we used to think. We can never go back to the mentality we left behind, that kept us in bondage.

ACTIVITY 39

INSTRUCTIONS FOR ALL UTOPIA MEDITATIONS. (Skip if you already know what you are doing.)

We are going to stand up this time, which will help us to not fall asleep. We are going to spread our feet a little bit to maintain balance because I am going to ask you to close your eyes. So close your eyes and begin deep breathing. With each breath we are going to see light in and darkness out. At this moment we do not need to know what it is that we are exhaling. Just know that any low vibe energy that does not help you to be happy and healthy will now leave. Just trust the process and feel like you are inhaling life and exhaling death. Breathe in light, exhale darkness. Breathe in high vibe and exhale low vibe. As you are doing this I want you to see this light entering from your head and going all the way to the bottom of your spine and turning around up creating a big oval. As you do these, with your eyes closed, roll your eyes backwards. (This is a hypnosis tool.) Do these as long as you need and let it all go.

Begin focusing on your face, relax your forehead and then relax your jaw. Move to your neck and shoulders and consciously relax them. Repeat all this until you end up relaxing your toes. Take your time and do not continue until you believe you are as relaxed as you are going to get.

Once you are there, begin focusing on the next area up where the inner eye is and see the color "indigo". I am going to ask for you to visualize yourself at your actual age with your physical eyes closed and your inner or third eye

SETTING MYSELF FREE FROM MY OWN MIND.

very open in the middle of your forehead. I want you to see yourself with a high level of intuition and acting on it with exceptional results.

See yourself totally connected with your heart at all times and listening to your gut feeling at all times before taking any decision. I want you to see yourself and your loved ones in a higher dimension. You can imagine or visualize all of them in their light bodies; it is still ok if you see all with physical bodies, if that helps. It is your vision, there is never wrong or right, or any limitation at all. Whatever works for you is good.

I also want you to see yourself easily being connected with your spirit and listening to higher truth or wisdom that sets you free instantly. I want you to see yourself full of power and getting rid of all low vibration collected from your past and your programming of the subconscious mind.

I want you to see an indigo light going through all your cells and delivering or downloading nothing but truth and health. I want you to see or imagine an open book with an indigo light in it. I want you to see yourself entering to a room of your choice, opening this book and reading. As you read I want you to see yourself receiving all higher truth in regards to all your struggles or questions.

Watch yourself seeing everyone around you as they are, not as you see them with your physical eyes. See them as light and love, and maybe acknowledging that most do not know who they really are. See you as loving and patient as can be to those still in ignorance.

See yourself full of wisdom, light and higher truth; see yourself being a light to others. See yourself loving all without any judgement, since you deeply know the higher truth about all humans; we are all one spirit of love in flesh.

Finish your meditation when you are ready and come back to it as many times as needed; as you feel totally comfortable and the new story coming easily to your mind

SETTING MYSELF FREE FROM MY OWN MIND.

like it really happened. End your meditation with the light in your spine and open your eyes when you are ready. Do this meditation three times a day for at least 7 days.

You can make these affirmations too: "I feel creative and inspired at all times. I listen to my intuition and I am always right- my body does not lie. I see the bigger picture. I do not search for my thought for truth. I search my spirit for wisdom. I do not look for answers outside myself. I look within. I am connected to my deeper self at all times. I am my own best friend and I trust my wisdom within. I enjoy deep relationships. I open my mind and learn at all times. I need to search for higher truth within if I am not experiencing peace within. I am calm and self-aware. I possess foresight. I make wise decisions based on my inner wisdom, the kingdom is within. I create my reality. I trust my intuition. I see with clarity. I trust myself. My mind and my heart are one". Whatever works for you, is perfect!

40 THE CROWN CHAKRA

The crown chakra is located at the top of our head. It is said that we are connected to the divine through our crown chakra. As mentioned before, the seven chakras are the energy centers in our body. The bottom, being the root chakra, that connects us with the physical world and the crown chakra that connects us to the spiritual world. Either way, in order to have a balanced life, we need to have all chakras balanced. And I cannot help to notice that purple is the color of the crown chakra which happens to be the combination of red and blue. This chakra system connects us to both the material and spiritual realms. The lower we go, the more physically we are connected, the higher we go the more spiritually we are connected. But the goal is not to be a super spiritual being without the heavenly life on earth. I used to escape emotional pain through meditation. To me this is not our goal. The goal of writing this book was to effortlessly achieve a balanced happy life while we are still here on earth.

I asked you to change or do something in every other chakra that we have studied so far. In this chakra there is nothing to change. I believe this chakra to be actual divinity, our Spirit. Can you change, improve or heal divinity (Spirit)? No, divinity is perfection and wholeness. There is zero lack in divinity.

With this said there is nothing we can do to fix this chakra. This chakra is already perfect. It is our awareness of who we really are that will open our crown chakra. If we totally believe there is a chakra in the top of the head that is totally divine, would you not go there for the solution to any of your struggles? Would you not stop going anywhere else but inside of you? Yes. The problem

SETTING MYSELF FREE FROM MY OWN MIND.

here is that they told us there was a god out there that could heal all our struggles, if we prayed hard enough or convince many others to pray for us. We should have been taught that there is divinity inside of us and the way to find answers is to go within and find wisdom/higher truth that could set us free.

Did they not say that the temple of god was within? Yes, they taught us that we are the temple of god, but they failed to teach us how to enter into the presence of god within. I remember, as a Christian, the long hours we spent worshiping a god out there so we could feel his presence. Little did we know that the actual presence of the divine is the top energy center in our heads.

I will explain what the crown chakra is to me, so you can effortlessly begin to embody your own divinity on earth, producing a life of bliss. Or what I call: effortless joy and peace.

Our crown chakra allows us to see the divinity in all things and allows us to be aware of our oneness with the entire universe. It is through higher truth that we become aware (conscious) of who we are and our power. As we acknowledge that our crown chakra is all Divine Wisdom, we will find all we need and think we lack. It is through this chakra that we become enlightened as we listen to this higher truth that sets us free, in other words, the increase of our consciousness. It is through the crown chakra that we can effortlessly embody our higher self and effortlessly experience serenity and bliss.

I do believe that meditation plays an important role on searching for Wisdom within. Meditation, used all over the world, is not magic; it's a tool that enables us to quiet the physical mind and enter Divine Wisdom itself. It is through love that we enter, and through the gate of the throat chakra, using mantras to keep left hemisphere busy. Passing through the third eye chakra and opening the gates, so all divinity can flow in the rest of our charkas to be healed, not only physically but emotionally. This is

SETTING MYSELF FREE FROM MY OWN MIND.

when we finally become one body, and not two.

ACTIVITY 40

I want you to reach the altered state of the mind, using any meditation technique of your choice. I want you to visualize your body. I want to see your physical body from the outside and the inside. I then want you to focus on your crown chakra as a purple light. I want you to see this light as bright as possible. I want you to see this light growing and getting brighter. Know that this light is divine and has the power to do anything your heart desires.

I want you to see this purple light going into all of your other six chakras balancing them, becoming alive and healthy. Know that, as this bright purple light is passing through all your other chakras, it is bringing Divine Wisdom with it and healing all that still needs to be healed. This light has the power to bring truth and erase lies from your entire existence, since the day you were born, as it reaches the root chakra.

I then want this purple light to embody your entire physical body, entering all of your cells and bringing this Wisdom and health to all of your cells. Be aware that this light has the power to heal and make everything new. Feel the pleasure, enjoy and stay here as long as you need.

I want you to then see your body, not just physical but also spiritual. See your body as physical and light at the same time. Then go ahead and see this purple light getting bigger than your physical body, creating an aura that will shine everywhere you go.

End the meditation when you are ready and whether you are aware or not, this is who you are: One body physical and light/Spirit, made one.

Pay close attention to the wisdom you will be receiving in the days to follow.

SETTING MYSELF FREE FROM MY OWN MIND.

It is our awareness of the truth that sets us free.

41 ONE LIFE, NOT TWO – ONE BODY, NOT TWO

You do not have two bodies but one. If you could have a physical body separate from a Spiritual (LIGHT) body then you would have two bodies, we would be back to square one with a theology of dualism (two). This theology of two bodies effortlessly produces a state of the mind which allows for the physical body to be sick and the spiritual body to be healthy. In other words, we remain sick and in bondage.

First I had to learn that I was one within: that god/divinity and myself are one, so it wasn't possible for me to feel a certain way and to feel god/divinity a different way. (All feelings and desires are pure and are here to show me something.) Now, I also had to come to the understanding that I had one body and not two. Not my body and the divine/light body in me, but one. There is no possible way that I can be sick and healthy at once if I have only one body. (The Spirit is always in a state of perfection).

Once we can see this and we deeply believe it, effortless health will manifest in our bodies. Remember, the fastest way to replace the lies (theology of dualism) with the truth that sets us free, is through receiving a revelation from Spirit in our mind. How can we achieve this? Yes, you know what I am going to say, "Through meditation".

"Wait a minute, are you telling me that I can receive divine health and eat junk for the rest of my life?", you might add. Allow me to clarify. Higher truth will always set us free, and it all begins with our thinking. Once we know and understand who we are, we will want to treat our bodies like if they were divine and important. Would you feed junk to a divine body? I do not think so. There are better chances that our self-healing body will do its job if we respect ourselves and our bodies. The manifestation of our higher reality does not come to pass until we deeply believe it, and act accordingly. Not honoring your feelings and not taking care of your body will never bring heaven on earth manifestation.

What about DNA and hereditary diseases? I believe that genes are not destiny. I think it all matters, environmental influences, nutrition, stress and emotional distress, but we are not powerless. I think, it is the generic traits and behaviors that are usually inherited too. So the question could be, "What triggers our generic traits that could manifest a health problem?" Would it not be a good idea to begin by exercising and eating properly if diabetes runs in your family? Are we really that powerless? It all starts with knowledge, I think. It has been clear for a while about the connection between refined sugar and disease. So why are we not looking at our labels? And why do we think we are powerless against diabetes? It all matters.

We do not experience two lives, but one. We do not live a carnal life every day and then a spiritual life once we are in meditation (or when we die). There should be one life of the divine human. The more we embody our spiritual body during meditation, the more we operate with the spiritual mind during our daily lives. As we **know** the truth, it just continues to flow through our mind and heart, as we live our daily lives. We begin to trust all our thoughts, feelings and intuitions, living effortlessly and experiencing Wisdom at all times. When asked a question we do not say, "Wait, let me go meditate/pray and I will tell you what I hear." The more time we spend living the one human/divine life, the more we are effortlessly embodying or manifesting divinity on earth. We begin to

SETTING MYSELF FREE FROM MY OWN MIND.

say what comes to our mind and heart at all times, only to discover we are Wisdom and Light, personified.

BECOMING YOUR HIGHER SELF- SHINING ON EARTH

As explained before, there is only one realm and not two. It is the same realm with different vibrations or dimensions. Just because we are unable to see something with our physical eyes doesn't mean it isn't there.

Our cell phones use electromagnetic frequencies that we can't see, this doesn't mean they aren't there. As we raise our vibrations we are opening ourselves to experience higher dimensions where we see and perceive it all through a different lens. The veil of illusion lifts and we see everything through the eye of our Higher Self.

How exactly do we become one with, or embody our Higher Self? The answer is simple and not hard to achieve either. As we continue to listen within, and are aware of our divine chakra, our life will begin to effortlessly show our true identity. It is not a matter of changing our life, it is a matter of changing our mind (awareness) or the way we think.

The more we listen during meditation, the more attuned we become to the voice of our higher self through our feelings and intuition the rest of the day. The more we will embody our higher being. It is through our consciousness or awareness of the truth that we effortlessly just become ourselves and be.

This chakra is not about work, it is about being aware we have divine wisdom within and the more this wisdom changes our mind, the more we embody divinity and the more we effortlessly create heaven on earth. We do not need to try and be divine, we just are divine and all we need to do is "be". It is our own authenticity that sets us free.

SETTING MYSELF FREE FROM MY OWN MIND.

RAISING OUR OWN VIBRATION. AS ABOVE, SO BELOW

Now we know we are one and not two. There is nothing that happens in the spiritual realm that does not have a consequence on earth. There are consequences for our flesh body and our life that happen effortlessly when we embody our higher self or light body. We will continue to experience fragmentation or separation if we continue to believe that we have two bodies (a spirit/light body and a separate flesh body). Even if it is hard to swallow in our carnal minds, the truth is we only have one body: 100% flesh and a 100% spirit or light body (for now, while on earth). Simply acknowledging this raises my vibration and gives me a physical tingling feeling.

Our higher self or spirit self (whichever you decide to call it), already *is* at the highest vibration possible. That is why we can't see it, because, in the flesh on this earth, we are vibrating at a lower flesh vibration so we can be solid and see a solid 3D world. The higher the consciousness, the higher the vibration we experience in our flesh bodies. In other words, the more we are aware of who we are, the higher the vibrations we experience on earth and the more we experience the spiritual realm during our meditations or travels with visions and trances. This will end up producing miracles in our earthly life and bring us closer to fulfilling our purpose here. So how exactly can we raise our vibration to effortlessly experience heaven on earth in all areas of our lives? Acknowledge higher truth and act accordingly.

ACTIVITY 41

HOW CAN WE SEND LIGHT/LOVE/HEALING TO OTHERS?

SETTING MYSELF FREE FROM MY OWN MIND.

Get yourself into the relaxed state of mind and visualize yourself as a physical body and purple light as one, as previously described in activity 40. Remember, there are no limitations to what you can imagine and produce with the power of your love-intentions. You can visualize your purple light body, having a ray of light that goes all the way to the center of earth.

This same ray of light goes as high as reaching the entire universe. You can now see yourself as a purple light body extending all your light to all planet earth, including your loved ones.

Your subconscious mind will be aware that you are the carrier of purple healing light once you begin to see a difference in your own health. I invite you to touch others and lay hands on them. Expect a tingling sensation. See what happens.

SETTING MYSELF FREE FROM MY OWN MIND.

42 UTOPIA MEDITATION

We not only know the Truth, we begin to be awakened to the reality that we ARE the Truth, when this chakra is awakened and balanced. It is here where we begin to embody our higher self. In other words, we become the walking TRUTH or the LIGHT. After we begin to be aware of our divine power we begin to effortlessly manifest heaven on earth. This is where we finally know that we are ONE, not only with god/divinity/wisdom, but with ONE another and the entire COSMOS, and that there is nothing that is not ONE.

People may start to label you a "lunatic" as they did with Jesus, because you see the truth that not everyone sees. For you the veil has been removed. What seems logical and true to you seems like blasphemy to others. It is here where we not only know and seek for Wisdom; we begin to embody Wisdom itself. We become new, healed, and one WITHIN. There are no more lies; there is no more power struggle within. We finally become one with our inner child. This is where we LOVE who we are and we become unstoppable.

This is when life becomes bliss. All we have to do is just BE and things happen. Not only do we hear wisdom and guidance, we begin to follow our feelings and inner intuition, we always know what to do. We become so united (ONE) with spirit/divine/wisdom that the right thoughts just come to mind; trusting these thoughts allows heaven to be manifested in our lives. We enter into enlightenment or divine consciousness when we activate our crown chakra, and union with the COSMOS.

We do not have a divine chakra within; we do not have

SETTING MYSELF FREE FROM MY OWN MIND.

Jesus or God within. At the same level that we acknowledge that we are divine in flesh, the same level of divine manifestations.

ACTIVITY 42

INSTRUCTIONS FOR ALL UTOPIA MEDITATIONS.
(Skip if you already know what you are doing.)
We are going to stand up this time, which will help us to not fall asleep. We are going to spread our feet a little bit to maintain balance because I am going to ask you to close your eyes. So close your eyes and begin deep breathing. With each breath we are going to see light in and darkness out. At this moment we do not need to know what it is that we are exhaling. Just know that any low vibe energy that does not help you to be happy and healthy will now leave. Just trust the process and feel like you are inhaling life and exhaling death. Breathe in light, exhale darkness. Breathe in high vibe and exhale low vibe. As you are doing this I want you to see this light entering from your head and going all the way to the bottom of your spine and turning around up creating a big oval. As you do these, with your eyes closed, roll your eyes backwards. (This is a hypnosis tool.) Do these as long as you need and let it all go.

Begin focusing on your face, relax your forehead and then relax your jaw. Move to your neck and shoulders and consciously relax them. Repeat all this until you end up relaxing your toes. Take your time and do not continue until you believe you are as relaxed as you are going to get.

At this time, I am asking you to focus on the crown of your head and see purple. I want you to visualize you are the purple light on the top of your head. I want you to stay there and feel. Feel the joy, the peace, and the wholeness of your being; embellish yourself in the feeling of Love and Wholeness. Stay there as long as you desire. The use of some crown chakra meditation music can be helpful.

SETTING MYSELF FREE FROM MY OWN MIND.

End your meditation with the light in your spine and open your eyes when you are ready. Do this meditation three times a day for at least 7 days.

SETTING MYSELF FREE FROM MY OWN MIND.

SETTING MYSELF FREE FROM MY OWN MIND.

43 THE END

This is the end of our journey together. It is not a "one day healing method"; it is a process for life. Just know that if you learn to find wisdom within, you will never ever have to find a guru to help you. You are your own guru and the only one that can set you free.

What I want to do in this chapter is an activity that will take a while in the beginning but with practice you will be able to do it in just a few minutes.

ACTIVITY 43

I want you to do a one "utopia meditation" with all chakras. I want you to visualize the day you were born up till today, seeing you personifying your higher being at all times. With the help of your imagination we are going to visualize the life we would have had if we lived in heaven on earth (utopia) and every one was aware of our true love reality. Remember this is not a lie, this is just being aware of a higher dimension and the new reality of our life. Our subconscious mind will be effortlessly programmed as you see your utopia perfect life, from day one until today. Do this meditation for as long as you need it.

I explained this meditation on YouTube. Feel free to watch. https://youtu.be/ RHZN78-MRo

All my love to you,
Bea Musick

SETTING MYSELF FREE FROM MY OWN MIND.

SETTING MYSELF FREE FROM MY OWN MIND.

44 CLOSING

It has been my pleasure for being allowed to show you the way to healing, the path to your own heart. It is by being YOU that will lead the way to continued healing not just for you but for those around you. Thank you again, Love.

OTHER BOOKS BY THE AUTHOR

- Oneness
- Gays are not going to hell
- Levels of awakening

SETTING MYSELF FREE FROM MY OWN MIND.

SETTING MYSELF FREE FROM MY OWN MIND.

A NOTE FROM THE EDITOR: JACK RAVES

Dear readers,

First of all, a huge thank you, Beatriz, for your book.... For your lessons and directions, activities included, to help finding ways to set our minds free.

Thank you for your confidence and trust in me. It came as a shock to me when you told me you accepted all my suggestions and changes, copying them directly into your own pages...

Most books in this genre have prologues, forewords, dedications and recommendations from (often) famous authors. Beatriz Musick's book is no exception of course. Just kidding...

My help -with the editing- lies within one of the chapters: following your dream, which, by the course of my life, did not turn out as I then wished.

I wanted to be a teacher of the English language (not an English teacher, I am Dutch). Went to private education which was interrupted for too long a time. Maybe I could have caught up later on, my life and career went into a different direction.

After a lifetime of practicing, (talking and writing) more than a lot, with friends from all over the world, I felt encouraged to take part in this very special book, editing a few lines in quite a few chapters.

I do realize that any well-educated reader, who has, better grip on language and expressions than me, will laugh at some of my editing. Most importantly, all readers who know English will surely be able to understand Beatriz' important message. I am sure you will get her message!

SETTING MYSELF FREE FROM MY OWN MIND.

Some of you, when reading my foreword, will say -or think- that this is about me and not about the book...You are absolutely right. I respect your opinion(s) and ideas.

This book is about ,setting free, is about being yourself. Well: to me this is being ME, another lesson that have I learned: the book ,speaks for itself...

Enjoy reading, set your minds free, like she did. Am working on mine, I AM

Jack

www.ingramcontent.com/pod-product-compliance
Lightning Source LLC
Chambersburg PA
CBHW031258110426
42743CB00040B/734